A Genealogist's Guide to
Discovering Your Female Ancestors

A Genealogist's Guide to

DISCOVERING YOUR
Female
ANCESTORS

Special strategies for uncovering hard-to-find information about your female lineage

Sharon DeBartolo Carmack

BETTERWAY BOOKS
CINCINNATI, OHIO

A Genealogist's Guide to Discovering Your Female Ancestors. Copyright © 1998 by Sharon DeBartolo Carmack. Printed and bound in the United States of America. All rights reserved. No part of this book may be reproduced in any form or by any electronic or mechanical means including information storage and retrieval systems without permission in writing from the publisher, except by a reviewer, who may quote brief passages in a review. Published by Betterway Books, an imprint of F&W Publications, Inc., 1507 Dana Avenue, Cincinnati, Ohio 45207. (800) 289-0963. First edition.

Other fine Betterway Books are available from your local bookstore or direct from the publisher.

02 01 00 99 98   5 4 3 2 1

Library of Congress Cataloging-in-Publication Data

Carmack, Sharon DeBartolo.
    A genealogist's guide to discovering your female ancestors / Sharon DeBartolo Carmack.—1st ed.
        p.   cm.
    Includes bibliographical references and index.
    ISBN 1-55870-472-8 (alk. paper)
    1. United States—Genealogy—Handbooks, manuals, etc. 2. Matrilineal kinship—United States. 3. Women—United States—Genealogy. 4. Genealogy. I. Title.
CS14.C38   1998
929'.1'082—dc21   97-48297
                                                                          CIP

Edited by Carol Mahan
Production edited by Saundra Hesse
Interior designed by Pamela Koenig and Angela Lennert Wilcox
Cover designed by Angela Lennert Wilcox
Cover photo provided courtesy of Robert and Ruth Terbrueggen

*It seems only natural to dedicate this book to
my foremothers; however, there are two living women
to whom this book is especially dedicated:*

*my mother
Mary Louise (Fitzhugh) Bart*

and

*my daughter
Laurie Ann Carmack*

Table of Contents

ACKNOWLEDGMENTS

In the course of researching and writing this book, I have incurred many debts. Several colleagues and friends read the manuscript at different stages: Katherine Scott Sturdevant, M.A.; Roger D. Joslyn, Certified Genealogist, Fellow of the American Society of Genealogists; Anita Lustenberger, C.G.; Suzanne McVetty, C.G.; Jayne Richardson, M.A.; and Susan Rust, B.A. Each one offered helpful comments. In particular, Anita Lustenberger read the draft at two different stages, for which I am grateful, and Jayne Richardson offered invaluable suggestions about the structure and readability of the book. For guiding me on research sources with which I was unfamiliar, I wish to thank Gordon Remington, Fellow of the Utah Genealogical Association; Marsha Hoffman Rising, C.G., F.A.S.G.; and Anita Lustenberger. Of course, I remain responsible for any errors in fact.

Five professional genealogists graciously supplied case studies for inclusion in the chapter on determining maiden names and parents: Anita Lustenberger; Ann Lainhart; Marcia Wyett, Certified Genealogical Record Specialist; Glade I. Nelson, Accredited Genealogist; and Roger D. Joslyn. Marcia Wyett also supplied examples of some land and pension records.

I would also like to thank Betterway Books for suggesting I write on this topic. Researching and writing this book has given me a new area of academic and professional pursuit.

To all of the women's historians, who have shared their research and knowledge through books and articles, I owe my appreciation for giving me ideas for sources on researching women and for enlightening me on all the fascinating topics in women's history.

Finally, my never-ending appreciation is due to my husband, Steve, and daughter, Laurie, for their patience and understanding, as I become obsessive-compulsive when writing a book.

Introduction

Ordinary, everyday women—the ones who are our ancestors—led fascinating lives. While the majority were law-abiding citizens whose lives revolved around home and family, there were also the intriguing women who grace people's family histories: Dorothy Talbye who murdered her three-year-old daughter, Difficult, in 1683; Nancy Bane who was confined to a cell in an insane asylum in 1868; Caroline, a plantation slave in Virginia, who had little, if any, control over her own life; Harriet Symonds who died from an abortion in 1850; Mary Stuart Fitzhugh, an 1840s Southern plantation widow, who may have been an opium addict; and Sarah Wheeler Cope who petitioned the county court for a divorce in 1772 because her husband had contracted the French Pox from carnal knowledge with lewd women.

Every woman led a life worth researching and recording; but not every woman created voluminous records. If you find murderers, lunatics, criminals and victims among your female ancestry, you are lucky. They are the ones who generated more and unusual records. The majority, however, were like Mary Ann (Davidson) Goforth, who had all she could manage: helping on the family farm, raising a large family and coping with her husband's disability after the Civil War. She was too busy with domestic life to get herself into trouble and create records. Yet her story deserves telling just the same. How do you research and write about her or the countless others like her who are your ancestors? The research sources and strategies in this book are designed to help you with this problem and others, such as determining maiden names and parents. There is a wealth of material out there for researching all types of women.

The Silent Woman

When I read published genealogies or receive information from other researchers, I am constantly amazed: Many of the women in the lineage are sorely neglected. There's generally a woman's name—sometimes her maiden name is known, sometimes it is not—and usually there are approximate birth and death dates for her. But this is about all. Here is an example from a typical family history (names have been changed):

> Samuel Billington was married in Franklin County, Ohio, on 20 January 1845 to Jenny Pollard. Jenny was born in Virginia on 9 April 1821 and died of a "complication of diseases" near Groveport, Ohio, on 16 November 1887.

Or worse:

> Jenny (—?—) Billington was born about 1821, probably in Virginia. She died in 1887 in Ohio.

Not only do these summaries put the reader to sleep, nothing here tells me what Jenny was like: how she might have dressed, what she did on a daily basis, how she felt about her life. While the preceding and following paragraphs of this family history go on and on about Samuel—what land he owned, his military service, his community activities—this is the only mention of Jenny, other than she was named in her husband's land deeds and his will. Was her life so unimportant that the most significant events for which she will ever be remembered were the day she was born and the day she died?

This neglect is somewhat understandable in the majority of family histories. In researching females, we have to deal with name changes when they marry, multiple marriages resulting in multiple names, or different cultures whose women retained their maiden names in legal documents. In addition, many of our women ancestors did not leave much of a record of themselves, especially when you consider they have been treated throughout most of history like children, with few legal rights (discussed more in Appendix A). The vast majority of women were silent partners. It was primarily the men who purchased the land, served in the military, were taken to court, signed as witnesses to documents, paid taxes, filed for citizenship and left wills. We consider ourselves lucky if we find a female ancestor named in the documents created by her husband or father. If she lived after 1850, we might find some detailed information about her in federal population censuses or other records.

Is she doomed to be silent forever? Is this to be her only legacy—a name on a chart?

It is inexcusable how our women ancestors have been overlooked in our genealogies—deprived of the narratives that tell about their lives. Half of all our ancestors were women. Each woman on our pedigree chart gives us a new surname and family line to pursue. Women were the shapers of the family. They carried on family traditions, passing on their culture learned from their mothers to their daughters. They bore the babies and risked their lives in childbirth. They raised the children and imparted moral values. They doled out much of the discipline. They were their children's first teachers. They ran the household, doing the cooking, cleaning and washing. They nursed the sick and prepared the dead for burial. Those who could read and write recorded life's events in letters, diaries and family Bibles. They may have added to the family income by selling eggs and butter, doing sewing and laundry, or opening their homes as boardinghouses. Women formed friendships with neighbors and started local civic organizations.

Exploring Women's Social History

An important and crucial source in your genealogical research on your female ancestors is women's social history. Besides helping you to understand your ancestors' actions and motivations, social history will augment and supplement what you find in the historical documents on your women. It can also fill the gaps left by records or where there are no records of your female ancestors.

Social history research combined with genealogical research will enable you to write a biography about your female ancestors. Instead of the highlights of her life being the day she was born and the day she died, you can write a narrative about her that will be one hundred times more interesting to read:

> Traveling for Emma Manyik was not a new experience. Born in Czechoslovakia in the 1830s, she had arrived in America by 1850. No doubt her voyage to America and then her trek to Illinois did not fully prepare her for what she would experience in her journey across the plains of Kansas five years later, pregnant and with two small children in tow. Caught up

in the westward migration fever that swept the nation, her husband, William, like so many other men of his times, made the decision to move his family to the western frontier. The opportunity to strike it rich and buy large tracts of land inexpensively was too much to pass up, and it beckoned people of all socioeconomic backgrounds. For women like Emma, however, who were in the midst of their childbearing years, the fever to move west could not have come at a worse time.

This is family history. This is Emma's real legacy. Her life has substance; it has meaning. She was a part of history. She wasn't just a name on someone's pedigree chart. The research is only half of the fun of genealogy—telling a forgotten woman's story is the rewarding half, giving you a real sense of accomplishment.

Writing Your Female Ancestors' Stories

Researching and writing about women is exactly like my mom's recipe for apple pie.

Mom's Recipe for Apple Pie
Step One: Ingredients
  9-inch double-crust pie pastry
  6 cups peeled Macintosh apples, sliced
  1 cup sugar
  3 tablespoons flour
  1 teaspoon cinnamon
  ½ teaspoon nutmeg
  Dash salt
  1 tablespoon butter

Step Two: Combine Ingredients

Heat oven to 425°. Prepare pastry. In large bowl, combine apples, sugar, flour, cinnamon, nutmeg and salt. Toss lightly to mix. Turn into pastry-lined pie pan. Dot with butter. Cover with top crust (cut slits for steam to escape). Seal and flute the edges.

Step Three: Bake

Bake for 40 to 45 minutes or until juice begins to bubble through the slits in the crust.

First you gather the ingredients. But each ingredient alone does not make an apple pie. You go to the second step and combine the apples, flour, sugar and spices. But this is still not an apple pie. You have to go to that final step, baking, where all the ingredients combine and blend together. That's apple pie.

Sharon's Recipe for Researching and Writing About Female Ancestors

Step One: Ingredients

> letters
>
> diaries
>
> oral history
>
> home sources and artifacts
>
> census schedules
>
> wills and probate
>
> medical records
>
> land records
>
> church records
>
> vital records
>
> school records
>
> social histories

Step Two: Combine Ingredients

Review and analyze all records pertaining to your female ancestors, their families, associates and friends. Add the relevant social history. Mix together family and social history until well blended.

Step Three: Bake

Write a narrative biography of your female ancestors that is both a legacy and an interesting read.

The ingredients are all of the sources you consult in your research project. But the sources by themselves do not tell your ancestor's life story. In the second step, you analyze each record, comparing and combining information from each document with information from social histories. But this still is not your female ancestor's story. When you go to the final step, writing her biography, where all of the sources meld into an interesting narrative, then you have recorded her legacy.

For some researchers, however, writing may not be one of their strengths. If this is all that is stopping you from writing about your female ancestors, you might want to enroll in a creative-writing course at your local community college. Even though your goal is to write nonfiction biographies, the techniques you will learn and evaluations you will receive can only benefit this goal. Or you can engage the services of a genealogical editor to polish your prose. Or consider giving your research to a family-history ghostwriter. Keep in mind, the biographies you compose about your female ancestors do not have to be Pulitzer Prize-winning quality. The point is to leave a written narrative about your foremothers for the future. You do not have to be an accomplished writer to do that.

About This Book

This book is intended to take you from start to finish in researching genealogical and historical information about your female ancestors, then writing their stories. It is *not* intended to be a beginner's guide to genealogical research methods and sources in general. If you have not yet begun researching your family history, I recommend one of these basic guidebooks: Sandra Hargreaves Luebking and Loretto Dennis Szucs' *Family History Made Easy: A Step-by-Step Guide to Discovering Your Heritage*, Ralph Crandall's *Shaking Your Family Tree*, Emily Anne Croom's *Unpuzzling Your Past: A Basic Guide to Genealogy* or Val D. Greenwood's *The Researcher's Guide to American Genealogy*.

The examples used throughout this book are of real women of the past. In a few cases, names have been changed out of respect to living descendants, and these

are noted. Sources about individual women are either given as part of the text or can be found at the end of the book in the Notes.

Whether you are researching female ancestors in the 1600s or 1900s; in the American north, south, east or west; of black, red or white color; of German, Italian, English, Middle Eastern, Asian or Scandinavian heritage; of Jewish, Catholic, Protestant or pagan religion, this book will help you. The examples cover a variety of women throughout American history. Though your particular nationality, ethnicity or race of female ancestry may not be mentioned specifically, the research methods and many of the sources will still apply.

There are no more excuses for researchers to neglect their women ancestors. Yes, tracing females can be difficult and challenging; it is research that requires creativity and patience. But if you agree that your foremothers were just as much a part of your heritage as your forefathers, you will realize that their lives deserve equal treatment in your genealogical research and your family history writing. *Every* female ancestor has a story worth telling—and she waits silently for you to tell it.

CHAPTER ONE

Sources Created by Women

*[Diaries have] been an important out-
let for women partly because it is an
analogue to their lives—emotional,
fragmentary, interrupted, modest,
not to be taken seriously, private, re-
stricted, daily, trivial, formless, con-
cerned with self and endless at their
tasks.*

Mary Jane Moffat,
Revelations: Diaries of Women

No one can trace a maternal, or paternal, ancestry by looking at only one type of
record (censuses, for example) or by entering a name into a computer database. In the
world of genealogy, researchers trace their
ancestry by using a variety of source materials. There are two basic categories of
sources you will seek in the course of researching your female ancestors:

- those created by a woman herself
- those created about her

Women who wrote letters, kept diaries,
stitched quilts or samplers, recorded events
in the family Bible, or who tell us their life
stories during an oral history interview have
created a historical source. Unlike birth certificates, census enumerations and wills, which
were created by someone else about the
woman from information either she or another person provided, the sources discussed
in this chapter were created by women.

Female ancestors who were literate
likely kept a family Bible, wrote letters to
family and friends, or kept a diary or journal
of their activities and thoughts. If letters, diaries or a Bible have been handed down in
your family, you have a wonderful beginning to your family history. In these unique
sources, you may find family events recorded that you will not find anywhere else.
For example, an infant who was born in the
1700s and lived only three weeks may be
recorded in the family Bible and nowhere
else, making it the only record of the baby's
existence. Before reading and studying
these documents, it is a good idea to make
photocopies to work with rather than han-
dling the original documents; you will want
to preserve these for future generations. Of
course, the material contained in letters, diaries and the family Bible is invaluable to
your genealogical research and writing your
ancestor's biography.

Letters

Letters to other women usually contained
news items about births, marriages and

deaths in the family. Women who followed their husbands to the frontier wrote about these events to relatives back home. Here are some examples of things you may find. On 15 September 1890 Mary, a pioneer woman in March, South Dakota, wrote about the birth of her sister to a relative in Indiana:

> Well ma has a 10¾ lbs She Baby again.[1]

Women's letters may also contain fascinating gossip not found anywhere else. Mary wrote to the same relative on 28 February 1909:

> Edna is all right—able to dance all right at a stretch, but makes Tab do the washings. Ha Ha. You don't need to sympathize with her for loosing her baby for she was tickled to get rid of it so easy.[2]

Letters from women to men may also contain news items as well as information on daily activities. These might also give you clues into a couple's relationship. Some letters may be rather matter-of-fact, while others may be filled with longing and desire: Henry Rayner wrote to his wife, Mahala, of "gaz[ing] upon thy beauteous face and snatch[ing] the nectar kiss from thy sweet lips." Linda Peavy and Ursula Smith in *Women in Waiting in the Westward Movement* reconstruct several couples' lives through letters such as the correspondence between the Rayners.[3]

Love letters are, of course, some of the most interesting reading material. Mrs. Sarah Austin wrote many letters to her clandestine lover in the 1830s. In one instance, Sarah was leaving on a short trip from home and would be away from her lover's daily arrival of letters:

> Do not laugh at me as I bid you farewell somewhat solemnly and as if we were parting. Here I have lived in a sort of half presence of what I love. Here I have received your letters. Here hangs your picture. Here are a thousand things . . . which remind me that you are not all a dream.[4]

Why is it that if we discovered our mother was having a secret affair, we would be shocked? But if Great-Great-Grandma had an affair—now that's romance! If you have surviving letters in your family, be prepared to find some of those skeletons that make family history so interesting.

Diaries and Journals

Diaries tend to record people's feelings, while journals are more likely to enumerate activities and events, although the terms have been used interchangeably. Regardless of its name, diaries are the autobiographies of ordinary women, and these may be the only existing records of their personal lives. Along with genealogical material, diaries will give you a wonderful glimpse into a woman's daily life, her thoughts and her attitudes. She may also record her feelings on national events, such as a war or its impact on her, her family and her community. It was more common for women to keep diaries only during periods of emotional stress, such as times of war, when they moved away from family and friends, or when they were separated from their spouses (the husbands were out West in search of gold, for instance). Diaries may have been written with the knowledge that one day they would be shared, such as with travel diaries; these accounts were meant to be read by those left behind. Marie Bashkirtseff, who died at the age of twenty-four from tuberculosis, kept a journal that she intended for someone to publish after her death:

> What if, seized without warning by a fatal illness, I should happen to die suddenly! I should not know, perhaps, of my danger; my family would hide it from me; and after my death they would rummage among my papers; they would find my journal, and destroy it after having read it, and soon nothing would be left of me—nothing—nothing—nothing! This is the thought that has always terrified me.[5]

Women of the Quaker religion were encouraged to keep spiritual journals that were published and shared with other women. About three thousand were printed before 1725. Howard Brinton's *Quaker Journals: Varieties of Religious Experience Among Friends* and Luella Wright's *Literary Life of the Early Friends, 1650–1725* are two invaluable sources if you have Quaker ancestry; these books also list the whereabouts of surviving originals. Be aware, however, that these diaries were edited before they were published; any passages that were contrary to Quaker beliefs were eliminated.[6]

Many women who moved to the frontier kept travel diaries. Along with documenting births and deaths, they also recorded their daily tedious activities like washing, baking, unpacking and packing, the number of miles the family traveled, the presence or absence of grass for the cattle. This diary entry was written by Catherine Haun, who journeyed across the plains in 1849:

> Every heart was touched and eyes full of tears as we lowered the body, coffinless, into the grave. There was no tombstone—why should there be—the poor husband and orphans could never hope to revisit the grave and to the world it was just one of the many hundreds that marked the trail. . . .[7]

If you have a diary or journal by one of your female ancestors, you have a special source. Read carefully the notations on the diarist's birthday and at the beginning of the new year. These tend to be times of reflection and self-evaluation for the diarist. Also, as with the Quaker diaries mentioned earlier, be cautious of published diaries. Read the editor's introduction to determine if the diary has been published in its entirety. Some editors may choose to emphasize certain aspects of the diary, depending on the editor's goal. For example, Laurel Thatcher Ulrich's *A Midwife's Tale: The Life of Martha Ballard, Based on Her Diary, 1785–1812*, is not a full transcription of Martha Ballard's diary, but Robert and Cynthia MacAlman McCausland's *The Diary of Martha Ballard, 1785–1812* is.

Relatives' and Friends' Letters and Diaries

During the nineteenth century in particular, women spent more time with other women—relatives and friends—than they did with their husbands or other men. Relationships with other women were extremely important in a woman's daily life. Whether married or single, women preferred each other's company. After all, it was female relatives and friends who were there for important events in a woman's life: births, marriages and deaths. The friendships women established with each other usually lasted a lifetime. Many middle-class school girls formed friendships in adolescence that blossomed into a lifelong companionship. Even when the girls were separated because one family moved, they wrote each other and perhaps visited. Ever wonder how your great-grandmother met your great-grandfather who lived several counties away? Visiting a girlfriend in another county was a great way to meet new eligible men: brothers, cousins, friends of the family.

Even if the diaries or letters of an ancestor have not survived, perhaps these exist for one of her relatives or friends. Finding her relatives' and friends' diaries and letters can provide you with two important aspects:

- Letters and diaries written by your ancestor's relatives and friends may contain material about your woman ancestor.
- These letters and diaries will give you a glimpse into what your own ancestor's life was probably like, since her relatives and friends probably came from the same socioeconomic background as she.

Think about your own close friends; you share similar likes and dislikes and similar lifestyles. Your women ancestors were no different in making friends—these may be neighbors, relatives or classmates.

Finding Letters and Diaries

How do you discover if your woman ancestor has surviving letters or diaries, or if her friends and neighbors left any? The first step is to contact all of your relatives to see if they might have these documents. Then try placing a "query" or advertisement in one of the genealogical magazines such as *Everton's Genealogical Helper* (P.O. Box 368, Logan, Utah 84323) or *Heritage Quest* (P.O. Box 329, Bountiful, Utah 84011-0329) to see if some distant relative whom you haven't discovered yet has some treasures. Once you determine your ancestors' friends and neighbors from research, queries in magazines are a good way to find descendants of these people.

Also check the area where your woman ancestor and her neighbors lived. Write or visit the state historical society libraries or archives, or university and public libraries that may have local history or special collections. Ask them specifically if they have any "papers" (a catchphrase historians and archivists use for letters, diaries, etc.) for your ancestor or her relatives or neighbors. You may also want to consider placing an ad or writing a letter to the editor in the local newspaper where your ancestor resided to see if any descendants are still in the area who may have historical papers.

Keep in mind, however, that women's papers could end up virtually anywhere. The Tutt Library of Colorado College in Colorado Springs has the diary of Sophronia Helen Stone in its Special Collections. Her diary covers her overland journey from New Lebanon, Illinois, to Yreka, California, in 1852. Although Sophronia never lived in Colorado Springs or anywhere in Colorado, her diary was donated to the college by a part-time professor who taught at Colorado College in 1948–49.

So your woman ancestor who lived her entire life in Virginia may have kept a diary that is now in a library or historical society collection in New Mexico. Perhaps the descendant who inherited it lived and died in New Mexico, and the diary was given to a repository there.

How do you find these strays and whether or not a diary may exist in a repository? Start with the *National Union Catalog of Manuscript Collections* (*NUCMC*)—affectionately referred to as "nuck-muck." *NUCMC* has been published annually since 1959 by the Library of Congress. The Library requests repositories all over the United States to report to them their manuscript holdings. *NUCMC* may be found in reference departments of college and university libraries and in large public libraries. There is a two-volume set called *Index to Personal Names in the National Union Catalog of Manuscript Collections, 1959–1984* that is especially helpful.

Another reference guide is Andrea Hinding's *Women's History Sources: A Guide to Archives and Manuscript Collections in the United States*. Here is a typical entry:

Goltra, Elizabeth Julia.
Papers. 1853. 21 pp.
Univ. of Oregon Library, Special
    Collections.
Journal describing a journey across
    the plains from Mississippi to
    Oregon.

This reference guide also has a geographical index, which makes the guide useful for checking the area in which your ancestor and her neighbors lived.

Some other helpful sourcebooks are William Matthews's *American Diaries: An Annotated Bibliography of American Diaries Written Prior to the Year 1861* and his *American Diaries in Manuscript, 1580–1954*. Margo Culley's *A Day at a Time: The Diary Literature of American Women From 1764 to the Present* is an anthology with a comprehensive bibliography of women's diaries. (See other sourcebooks in the Bibliography.)

Letters and Diaries Written by Women Like Your Ancestor

Suppose you can't find a diary or letters for your ancestor or her relatives, friends or neighbors. Now you need to be looking for diaries of women *like your ancestor*: a woman who lived in the same time period and in about the same place. Let's go back for a moment and look at Sophronia Helen

Stone's diary that is found in the Colorado College library. She made the overland journey from New Lebanon, Illinois, to Yreka, California, in 1852. Here is what her diary contains, based on the cataloging description prepared by the librarians:

Sophronia Stone gives an excellent description of an overland journey. Through her words you can see, smell, hear, and feel what life was like traveling in a covered wagon across a strange land. She tells what food they ate and how it was cooked, how they used buffalo chips for fuel, and how they dealt with illnesses—such as cholera, measles, and mountain fever and the medicines used to combat them. She mentions the prices of food, how they slept, and the ferrying fees. She tells of river crossings and getting stuck in sloughs. She writes of the number of campfires in camp, the noises, camp meetings, and a grocery store along the trail. Sophronia describes almost all the important landmarks along the trail. She speaks of the horrible conditions of the roads, of encounters with Indians, Indian burial mounds, of a child's funeral, of quicksand, beaver dams, a prairie funeral, tombstone inscriptions, bible meetings, a family's murder, prairie justice, drownings, and Range escorts through dangerous Indian country.

Now suppose your ancestor left from about the same area and went to about the same place during the 1850s. Wouldn't Sophronia's diary help show you what the journey was like, even though it does not deal specifically with your own ancestor?

Emily French, a middle-aged, divorced, working woman in Colorado in 1890 wrote about "the people she worked for and met, with insights into their personalities, homes, and lifestyles" in her diary.[8] She writes about different foods she ate at meals, specific illnesses of friends, childbirth and funerals. Helen Banfield Jackson's diaries cover the time period 1876–99[9] and are filled with names of people she visited frequently. Maybe one of these people was your ancestor.

More and more women's diaries are being published. Women's historians often transcribe and annotate women's diaries found in repositories. One of the most famous recently published is Laurel Thatcher Ulrich's Pulitzer Prize-winning *A Midwife's Tale: The Life of Martha Ballard, Based on Her Diary, 1785–1812*. Martha Ballard kept a diary for twenty-seven years and attended 816 births; she named hundreds of men, women and children. She recorded these events as well as domestic life in Hallowell, Maine. In particular, if your ancestors were in this area between 1785 and 1812, you would want to consult this book and Robert and Cynthia MacAlman McCausland's *The Diary of Martha Ballard, 1785–1812*.

Sometimes portions of women's correspondence and diaries are published as an anthology, such as the book *Women in Waiting in the Westward Movement*, mentioned previously, or Lillian Schlissel's *Women's Diaries of the Westward Journey*.

You just never know where one of your ancestors or her relatives, friends or neighbors may show up.

Family Bibles

Women in the family were the ones most likely to record the family's vital statistics in a Bible. This is a good place to find evidence of births, marriages and deaths before the time when states mandated vital registration in the late nineteenth and early twentieth centuries. If you are researching a slave family, you may find slave births and deaths recorded in the plantation mistress's family Bible.

Search out family Bibles in the same manner that you would look for letters and diaries. Check with relatives first, then place ads in genealogical magazines. Sometimes other genealogists will advertise finding and buying an old family Bible at a garage sale, then they seek descendants to send it to. Also check repositories in the area where your ancestors lived. The Virginia State Library, for example, has a large collection of Bible records. Here's a sample entry from its *A Guide to Bible Records in the Archives Branch, Virginia State Library:*[10]

> Jeter Family, Amelia County, 1774–1954. Bible printed in 1854. Other surnames mentioned: Anderson, Corbin, Jones, Puryear, Weiser, and Worsham. This item includes slave births.

Men and women who applied for military pensions from the Revolutionary or Civil War, for example, had to prove births

of their children and their marriage. Many times, they tore out the pertinent pages from the family Bible since there was no way to make a photostatic copy back then. These pages, if submitted, can be found among pension files.

Another place to look for Bible entries is genealogical journals. Many state and national periodicals publish family Bible records. In order to find these, check the *Periodical Source Index* (*PERSI*), published annually and available at most genealogical libraries.

When you find a family Bible, also check through all of the pages. There may be prayer cards, letters, postcards or notations by meaningful passages. A word of caution about the accuracy of the information you find in a family Bible: Always check the date the Bible was published against the dates of births, marriages and deaths. If a Bible published in 1878 has entries that predate its publication, then you know the information was not recorded at the time of the event, but much later. In that case, the dates of these entries may not be entirely accurate.

Family Artifacts and Heirlooms

Sewing was part of women's daily work and pastime. Needlework such as quilts and samplers were sewn by both young and old women. Some of these artifacts may still exist in your family and give you genealogical clues. Sometimes the sampler was of the family tree. From the needlework style, you may be able to determine when the piece was created. Mary Jaene Edmonds's

Samplers and Samplermakers: An American Schoolgirl Art, 1700–1850, Susan Swan's *Plain and Fancy: American Women and Their Needlework, 1700–1850* and Barbara Brackman's *Clues in the Calico: A Guide to Identifying and Dating Antique Quilts* are helpful books on this subject.

Antique jewelry may also provide interesting material for your family history. Check all jewelry carefully for any inscriptions. Lockets may contain photographs or a lock of hair. Mourning jewelry was often created from the deceased's hair and made into rings, broaches and bracelets. Sometimes wreaths of hair are part of a family's heirlooms. The family's silver may also contain clues. It may be engraved with initials or a crest. The origins of these artifacts and the family stories that surround them are important to your women's family history.

Cookbooks may contain more than your ancestor's favorite recipe for making pies. You may also find recipes for home health remedies and cleaning agents, such as soap. Keep watch for any items in your home or your relatives' homes that may give you clues or information about your women ancestors. Here are some more examples: autograph albums, scrapbooks, clothes, dolls and toys, books and magazines, and kitchen utensils. See the Source Checklist in Appendix C for other home sources. Artifacts of all kinds can be woven into the narrative biography about your female ancestors.

Oral History

Oral history is an important part of any family history. Not only should you speak with your female relatives at the beginning of your family history project to get vital statistics, such as births, marriages and deaths, but you should also interview relatives as you gather information. Focus most of your interviews on the why, how and what. Why did your family move to Kansas? How did you manage during the Depression? What was it like to give birth at home with only a female relative in attendance?

Along with recording the family stories, ask women relatives what life was like growing up, becoming an adolescent, falling in love, getting married, having children. Depending on the relationship you have established with the person you're interviewing, you may also want to ask some personal and intimate questions, such as:

- How did you feel when you started your first menstrual period?
- How did your mother prepare you for marriage? For womanhood?
- What was your reaction when you learned you were pregnant for the first time? The last time?
- Did you use any forms of birth control to limit your family's size?

I remember my grandmother telling me about when her first period began. She had gone to a picnic, and when she went to the restroom, she discovered blood on her panties. Not having been told about menstruation, she thought she had sat on a piece of glass and cut herself!

Some other important questions to ask of any relative with whom you are conducting an oral history interview are:

- What has been your guiding philosophy in life?
- What has been your biggest regret in life?
- What words of wisdom would you like to pass on to your descendants? (When interviewing a woman, also ask, "What words of wisdom would you like to share with your female descendants?")
- What would you liked to be remembered for?
- What do you remember about your grandparents, and grandmother, in particular?

In these interviews, try to ask questions about daily life, impressions, thoughts and feelings, since these are areas that will be lost when a person dies. You won't find this information in any record.

Once you have interviewed your women relatives, broaden your scope to include female friends and neighbors of your relatives. They can give you a different perspective on your own relatives and ancestors.

Remember to also ask your female relatives about documents and artifacts they've gathered over their lifetimes: old letters, postcards, photographs, diaries, needlework, quilts, souvenirs, favorite recipes, favorite books or poems, and the family Bible.

When using oral history in a woman's biography, also put in some historical perspective. Here's an example:

My mother enjoyed working at the State House in the early 1900s. She had a large contingent of girlfriends who worked in the other offices. Like many women of her day, once she married Elliott in 1910, she quit her job to become a full-time housewife and mother.

By adding this simple phrase, "Like many women of her day . . . ," you show that her actions were common for that era. You can also supplement the interview with records. For instance, if during an interview your grandmother recalls being in San Francisco during the Great Earthquake of 1906, you can supplement her personal account with newspaper articles. Or, if she tells about life during the Depression, you can augment her experiences with social histories that discuss women's lives in general during the Depression.

All of the stories and information you gather are not only invaluable to your family history, but these details will be extremely useful when you are ready to write a narrative, biographical account about your female ancestors.

Legislative Petitions

This may seem like an unusual source to include in a chapter on sources created by women, but these are records that were indeed created by women: petitions for moral reform and woman suffrage that were submitted to state and national legislatures. Though the leaders in the woman suffrage movement were the women who made the history books, Elizabeth Cady Staton and Susan B. Anthony, they and their followers generated petitions to the New York legislature with more than ten thousand signatures of ordinary women in favor of suffrage and married women's property rights. Housed in the National Archives are also hundreds of thousands of women's signatures on petitions to Congress collected between 1834 and 1843 as part of female antislavery societies. The Women's National Loyal League, which also sought to abolish slavery, collected 400,000 signatures by 1865.[11] Along with petitions for abolition and suffrage, there were also petitions against polygamy, for setting aside public lands for the use of female academies, and for alcohol temperance. In addition to the names of the petitioners, these documents may also list the name of the woman's town or county of residence and an expression of her opinion on the problem.[12]

When a petition was sent to Congress, it was referred to an appropriate committee whose jurisdiction most closely matched the subject of the petition. According to the *Guide to the Records of the United States House of Representatives, 1789–1989*, "A major exception to this procedure was in the case of antislavery petitions presented during the antebellum period. According to a 'gag rule' in effect in the House from the 1830s through the 1850s, these petitions were neither received nor referred to a committee; however, many are extant among congressional records."[13]

The House and Senate records concerning petitions such as the ones described above are open to the public,[14] but in order to access these records, you will either need to visit the National Archives yourself or engage the services of a professional researcher. The petitions are not microfilmed, and there are no name indexes. In the Bibliography, I've included references to some of the most common petitions—abolition, temperance and suffrage—that should aid your search. According to the *Guide*, however:

> Researchers looking for all petitions from a particular locale on one topic or on many topics, face several problems. The indexers of the *Congressional Record* and its antecedents were not consistent in identifying the States from which the petitions were received. One means of surmounting this problem might be to examine petitions introduced by legislators from the locale under study, since most legislators tended to introduce petitions from their own district or State. . . . Further, petitions referred to each committee are usually arranged chronologically by the date introduced on the floor . . . but rarely are they arranged alphabetically by State or town.[15]

The *Congressional Record* (1873–present) is the official record kept of the proceedings in both the House and Senate and is indexed by subject and by bill and resolution number. Prior to the *Record*, the *Congressional Globe* (1833–73) was the authorized printer of congressional debates.

The House and Senate *Journals* (1789–present) are the only constitutionally mandated record of floor proceedings. These include the referral of petitions to committees, but they do not reproduce the debates and speeches. The *Journals* are indexed by subject and by bill or resolution number. These finding aids are available in the government documents section of some public and university libraries.

Because of the difficulty in accessing these records, unless you have reason to believe an ancestor signed one of these petitions or unless you just happen to be going to the National Archives, I would not put this source at the top of my research list. It is one you should be aware of, however, in case you do uncover from other sources that your female ancestor did sign a petition that was sent to the legislature. If you are planning a trip to the National Archives, or for more information about these records, you may write to the Center for Legislative Archives, National Archives and Records Administration, Washington, DC 20408.

———

Women created many types of sources that are valuable to genealogists and biographers. If you can locate letters and diaries, you have an extremely valuable source. Study these carefully for genealogical information, as well as details that you can use when you write a woman's biography. From home sources to petitions that ended up in Congress, many of our foremothers left records of themselves; it's up to you to find out if they still exist. The search is well worth your effort. Now let's look at some sources in the next chapter that were created about women.

CHAPTER TWO
Sources Created About Women

This history of women cannot be written without attention to women's relations with men in general and with "their" men in particular, nor without attention to the other women of their society.

Elizabeth Fox-Genovese

If historian Elizabeth Fox-Genovese were also a genealogist, she might add that the *genealogy* of women cannot be researched without attention to women's relations with men and other women of their society. Tracing specific women in historical documents can sometimes be easy; in other cases, it can take you on a journey into the records of everyone who came into contact with your ancestor.

Following the "rule" of genealogy—which is to start with yourself and work backward in time, or to go from the known to the unknown—you may have great success in finding records on your mother, grandmothers and perhaps great-grandmothers. The more recent documents of the late nineteenth and early twentieth centuries often contain quite a bit of information that deals specifically with a particular woman. A woman's death certificate, for example, may tell you her married name, her maiden name, her father's name, her mother's maiden name, her husband's name, the date and place she was born, the date and place she died, where she was buried and the cause of her death.

A twentieth-century passenger arrival list for Isabella (Veneto) Vallarelli gives the following data on her: her age (she was sixty-nine when she left Italy for America in 1916), her marital status (widow), her maiden name (Veneto), where she was born (Terlizzi, Italy), her occupation (housewife), her ability to read and write (illiterate), where she originated (Terlizzi, Italy), her closest relative still living in Italy (her brother Francesco Veneto), her final destination in America (Rye, New York), how much money she brought with her to America ($1,000), that she had never been to America before, the person she was joining in America (her son-in-law Salvatore Ebetino in Rye), that she was in good physical and mental condition, and her physical description (four feet tall, dark complexion, gray hair and brown eyes).[1]

The problems come as you work further back in time. Information in some records becomes scant, records have been lost or destroyed, and there is more attention to men in the records than women. This is due mainly to women's legal status and its changes throughout American history as discussed in Appendix A. Learning about the laws affecting women will enhance your research success.

Research Strategies

The main objective in researching women is to leave no stone unturned. You never know what record will provide you with information. And you never know what record about *someone else* will provide you with facts on your female ancestors. If you think of your grandmother, for example, in terms of some of her roles in life, you can broaden your research:

- daughter
- wife
- widow
- mother
- grandmother
- sister
- niece
- granddaughter
- friend
- neighbor

As a daughter: There may be mention of her in records on her father or mother, such as in wills. As a wife or widow: Check for all records of her husband that may likely name her, such as pension applications. As a widow: Her legal and social status changed, so she may create records under her own name. As a mother: Look for documents on her children, such as death certificates that give the mother's name. As a grandmother: She may be living with one of her grandchildren and can be found on a census in that household. As a sister: You may find mention of her in a sibling's diary. As a niece: She may be an heir to an unmarried uncle. As a granddaughter: She may inherit something from a grandparent. As a friend: She may be discussed in a letter. And as a neighbor: She may own the adjoining property and be named in a land deed.

Researching in Original Records

Another research point to keep in mind is that there are different records for different time periods and localities, so it is extremely important to learn the sources for that era and place. For example, you won't find federal census records prior to 1790, so if you are researching in the 1600s, that record is not a source for you. Likewise, if you are researching in Wyoming in the 1870s, you may find a voter registration on your female ancestor, since woman suffrage was passed there in 1869; but you won't find a voter list for women in Vermont until the Nineteenth Amendment was passed in 1920 (see Voter Lists and Registrations, page 26). You may find an index such as the Charles R. Hale Collection of the Connecticut State Library that records early cemetery inscriptions and newspaper notices for that state. Other states may not have such a collection.

It is beyond the scope of this book to discuss all of the different types of sources available, but in Appendix C you will find a detailed Source Checklist of common and uncommon records. General genealogical guidebooks as listed in the Introduction and

Bibliography will give you the background information you need to locate and use these historical records. The emphasis here will be on records that give you specific information on women. In addition, where applicable, I'll recommend social histories that complement a particular record that will give you supplemental material to use when you write a woman's biography (see chapter five).

Though you may not find each and every type of record on your women ancestors or their associates, the Source Checklist in Appendix C is provided to remind you of potential sources and to give you ideas for possible records. Never dismiss a record because you haven't heard any family stories or haven't discovered something in another record that would lead you to believe an ancestor would be in that document. For instance, many women petitioned for divorce, but it was never granted. A former client happened upon a divorce petition for her grandmother in the 1870s. Although the woman claimed extreme physical cruelty from her husband—being beaten, choked, whipped with an ox whip, and being threatened that he would get rid of her by chopping her head in two—the divorce was never granted.

You may discover from an obituary that your great-grandmother was a suffragist. Check police records. She may have been arrested during a demonstration along with hundreds of other women.

Or perhaps a female ancestor was one of the thirty thousand women shirtwaist makers who went on strike in New York City in 1909 for better wages and working conditions. Many of these women were arrested and incarcerated. A year later, 146 women were killed in a fire at the Triangle Shirtwaist Company. This shop refused to install fire escapes and kept workroom doors locked. Newspaper accounts would be invaluable if a female ancestor was part of these events.[2]

Or maybe one of your urban female ancestors worked in a birth control clinic at the turn of the twentieth century and was arrested. Margaret Sanger, founder of Planned Parenthood, certainly wasn't a hardened criminal, but she did spend a great deal of time behind bars for her progressive views.

Some Typical and Atypical Sources

Published Family Histories

Usually one of the first steps in researching either a maternal or paternal ancestry is to check to see if someone has already published a family history. If you are working with old New England families, you may very likely find a printed genealogy. If you are researching a recent immigrant or an ethnic minority, you may be the one to write and publish the family history. Be wary if you do find a published genealogy, however. Many are not documented and should only be used as clues. Even if you find a well-researched and documented family history, do some digging and check the original records yourself.

Family skeletons and overlooked clues may greet you in the records, but you probably won't find any mention of the skeleton in the published family history. Harriet (Symonds) Easton is an excellent example of the advantages of going beyond the published family history and looking at the records. She is listed as the wife of Agis Easton in *Descendants of Joseph Easton, Hartford, Connecticut, 1636–1899*, compiled by William Starr Easton in 1899.[3] This family genealogy records that Harriet was Agis's second wife, that they had no children and that she died at the age of twenty-seven on 23 March 1850. No sources are given for this information. Interestingly, the vital records for East Hartford, where Harriet died, do not list her death, but these do include the death of her daughter by Agis, also named Harriet, who died at the age of three weeks in September 1849.[4] Because Harriet Sr. died during a mortality schedule census year, 1850—deaths reported between 1 June and 31 May in 1849–50—perhaps the mortality schedule would give her cause of death. It did: *abortion.*[5] Although it is not clear why the family history does not mention the birth and death of Harriet Jr., we can certainly understand why Harriet Sr.'s cause of death would not have been included. An 1850 abortion, probably self-induced and occurring six months after the death of her first child, was not something someone in 1899 would want to publish in the family history (even if the compiler were aware of the cause).

Despite the flaws in some published family histories, these can save you hours of research and should not be overlooked. Just use them with caution, especially if they are undocumented.

Cemetery Records and Tombstone Inscriptions

The cemetery may sometimes be the only place where you will find proof that a female existed, especially if she died young. Mary Ann Hooe, daughter of Abram Barnes Hooe and Sarah Hornwood Johnson Hooe, was born 9 October 1815 and died 7 November 1816. She was buried in St. Paul's Episcopal Chapel Cemetery in King George County, Virginia.[6] This time period is too early for vital registration. Her birth and death fall between census years, so you won't find Mary Ann on any census. Further research may reveal a baptism record or a Bible entry; otherwise, this is it.

Cemetery transcribing projects are popular among genealogical societies, who make their work available in print to large genealogical libraries, such as the Family History Library in Salt Lake City, Utah. Though checking these compilations is quick and easy, always try to visit the cemetery yourself to see the tombstone. Family members may be buried not just alongside a girl or woman, but in the row in front or behind.

For young girls and unmarried women, the stone may be inscribed "daughter of . . ." For a married woman, it will more likely be inscribed "wife of . . . ," information you probably already knew. If you see "Sarah, *consort* of William Grimes," this means that she died before her husband. On the other hand, "Sarah, *relict* of William Grimes," would mean that he died before her, leaving her a widow.[7] Occasionally you will find a tombstone for a woman that reads "Mrs. Henry Smith." This, of course, is most disappointing, since it would appear that her only identity in life was in connection with her husband. Sometimes young wives who died within the first few years of marriage were buried with their own families instead of their husband's. If a mother and baby died during childbirth, they were usually buried together.

On some tombstones you may find a tile photograph embedded in the stone. This may be the only photograph still in existence. If cemetery records still exist, check with the sexton for these. They often give you more information than the tombstone and provide you with names of other relatives. In some cases, there may be only a burial record and no grave marker.

Make the most of cemetery research: Check first for published tombstone inscriptions if you do not live in the area where your ancestors were buried. If possible, try to visit the cemetery in person and also look for surviving burial records. Also, if your female ancestor became a widow, think about the impact this had on her life and how it would have changed.

Church Records

Church records are another source where you may find your female ancestors and nowhere else. If baptismal records exist for the church where you suspect an ancestor was baptized, look for these. These records can predate the recording of state birth certificates. Quaker women, in particular, were especially active in their religion. (See chapter one, Diaries and Journals, and chapter

five, Religion and Spiritualism.) Women participated in many church activities, so records of memberships and church groups would also benefit your search. Immigrant women of the late nineteenth and early twentieth centuries often felt comfortable socializing in church activities, where they could mix with women who spoke the same language and had the same moral and religious values.

Along with social histories on individual denominations to help you write a narrative, see Rosemary Ruether and Rosemary Keller's *Women and Religion in America* (three volumes), which covers, among others, Native American, African American, Southern, New England, Jewish and Catholic women. Look for items such as religious holidays and observances and how your ancestor would have celebrated these with her family. With special meals? With festivities? What was the religious doctrine? What activities or behaviors were considered inappropriate? Was there a punishment, and if so, what? How would she have practiced her religion (e.g., regular church attendance, involvement in women's groups, prayer meetings), and how would she pass her values on to her children (e.g., nightly Bible readings)?

Censuses

An enumeration of the population has been taken every ten years since 1790. The most recent census available for public search is 1920; 1930 will be released in 2002. The censuses between 1790 and 1840 list the name of only the head of the household;

sometimes this is a woman. The listing of the household's head is followed by a tally of males and females according to age. The 1840 census, however, also named Revolutionary War pensioners or their widows receiving pensions. Starting in 1850, everyone in the household (excluding slaves) is listed by name, and this is when you will begin to find more information on your women ancestors on the census. Certain censuses recorded specific questions that are beneficial to researching women. For example, 1850 asked of couples if they were married within that year; 1870 asked people if their parents were of foreign birth; 1880 asked for the parents' birthplaces (usually naming a state or country only) of everyone being enumerated; 1900 and 1910 asked the number of years a couple had been married, the number of children born to women and how many children were living. Many of these censuses also listed information on when a person immigrated to this country and the naturalization status (alien, declaration filed or naturalized).

Look carefully at the entries for all individuals in a woman's census enumeration and really study the information it gives you. Here are some questions you might ask yourself as you analyze censuses:

- Was her husband listed as disabled, perhaps from service in a war or from a farming accident?
- Were any of her children recorded as deaf or blind, idiotic or insane, or having another physical or mental handicap?

- Were there aged parents or other dependent relatives living in her home who may have posed a unique challenge to her daily routine?
- If the answer is yes to any of the above questions, consider how a woman's life was affected by any of these people with special needs. What additional stress and domestic duties would these circumstances entail for her and her family?
- Was there a domestic servant living in her household to aid her?
- How many children did she have and how closely spaced were their births? What toll did frequent births have on her health and well-being? If the births were spaced at wide intervals, could she have been using some form of birth control?
- How many of her children attended school, and how many stayed home with her during the day who needed watching and attention?
- If she was an immigrant who could not speak the English language but her children could, how did she communicate with them? In addition, how would she have felt about her children adopting American values that may conflict with her upbringing and culture?
- What might her social status have been, considering her husband's occupation and the value of his real and personal properties?
- If she was literate, what would her own education have been as a girl?

Would she have likely taught her children the basics of reading and writing before they attended school?

- Did her husband own slaves, and if so, what might her duties and responsibilities have been concerning them? How would she have likely felt about slavery?

- Were there mulatto slaves listed that could be her husband's offspring? How would she have felt about this common situation? How would she have treated the slave woman who had relations with her husband? How would she have treated the offspring?

- What was her ethnic background compared to her husband's? Were their cultures compatible? If not, how would they have likely dealt with the differences in areas such as religion?

- What customs, traditions and folkways from her cultural heritage would she have passed on to her children? What cultural holidays would they have celebrated?

- Did she or any of her daughters have occupations outside of the home? What impact would this have on the family?

- Who were the women living in the households listed before and after your female ancestor? Could these women have been her friends? Relatives?

Some of the answers to these questions will come directly from the information on the census; others will have to be researched in social histories, which will tell you the typical or common experience (see chapter five).

In addition to population schedules there are also special federal census schedules. Mortality schedules were taken in 1850, 1860, 1870 and 1880. If one of your ancestors died between 1 June and 31 May in 1849–50, 1859–60, 1869–70 or 1879–80, check these records. It was on the 1860 mortality schedule that I learned that twenty-eight-year-old Mary Dunavant and her five-year-old daughter Elizabeth died from burns in Giles County, Tennessee.[8]

In 1890 a special veterans enumeration was taken. Although the majority of 1890 population schedules and part of the veterans schedules were destroyed in a fire, those states alphabetically for half of Kentucky through Wyoming still exist. If your ancestor was a widow of a Civil War veteran, she will be listed. The census takers were supposed to enumerate only Union veterans and their widows, but often Southern sympathizers recorded those who fought for the Confederacy. Lines were later drawn through their names, but the information is still readable.

A little-used source is the 1880 Schedule of Defective, Dependent, and Delinquent (DDD) Classes. Many women spent some time in insane asylums. What we view today as manic depression, postpartum blues and menopause caused women of the past to be committed either permanently or temporarily. (See further discussion on insane asylums, page 35.) Mary Ann Vance was found on the 1880 schedule of DDDs; her first mania attack was at age forty-three, and she spent time in the Athens, Ohio, Insane Asylum.[9] Susan Mills was labeled as having dementia. Though she was discharged from the Athens Insane Asylum in 1878, she was still listed on the 1880 schedule of DDDs.[10] If a woman is listed as insane and currently an inmate of an insane asylum, check the regular population schedules for that institution for more information about her. Female ancestors may also be found in the DDDs under the headings for paupers in almshouses, in jails or prisons, as homeless children, or those who were blind, deaf or mute.

See Ruth Land Hatten's "The 'Forgotten' Census of 1880: Defective, Dependent, and Delinquent Classes" in the March 1992 issue of the *National Genealogical Society Quarterly* for availability of these schedules. Frederick Wines's *Report on the Defective, Dependent, and Delinquent Classes* gives informative and statistical information on this schedule that can be used when writing a narrative.

This section has only scratched the surface when it comes to census records. Other types of enumerations may be available depending on your area and time period of research: agricultural, business/manufacturing, school, church and state censuses, for example. (See chapter three for a discussion on slave and Native American censuses.)

Oh, and be cautious of women's ages in the decennial censuses. Some women aged only a few years in a ten-year period!

Passenger Arrival Lists

If your woman ancestor was an immigrant, seek out her passenger arrival list, if extant.

Many women came to the colonies as ex-convicts (petty thieves, prostitutes and vagrants) and indentured servants. A woman bound as a servant to someone who paid her passage worked off the indenture over a period of years, usually seven, unless she became pregnant during her indenture. Another year was generally added to her indenture to make up for the time away from work during her pregnancy.

Though this country has seen an influx of immigrants throughout its history, passenger arrival lists prior to the late nineteenth century contain scanty details about new arrivals. The passenger lists of the early twentieth century, however, offer the most information to genealogists. As mentioned earlier in the case of Isabella (Veneto) Vallarelli, the passenger list gave a great deal of data on her that may not be found elsewhere. Of particular importance when searching passenger lists is to know the customs and culture of the ethnic group you are researching. In some cultures, such as Catholic Italians and French, it was the custom for a woman to use her *maiden* name in all legal documents. Isabella was not recorded on the passenger list by her married name of Vallarelli, but her maiden name of Veneto. When a woman belonging to one of these cultures traveled with children, the children were listed by their father's surname, but the mother was listed by her maiden name. If you do not know her maiden name, look in the indexes for the children under their father's surname; you'll find her listed with them. (When you bridge the ocean and search records in foreign countries, remember that the death certificate of a woman who stayed in the homeland would also be listed under her maiden name.)

Just as you studied the information on censuses, look carefully at the information on passenger lists. Note especially all other immigrants coming from the same village as your ancestor, to see if these people become her neighbors or relatives. Also think about how her life would have changed being a foreigner in a strange land. How did she cope? How did she keep her culture alive? Did she learn to speak English? How would she have adapted to American life? Books on immigration in general and the immigrant experience will be helpful when writing about immigrant women. See works such as Roger Daniels's *Coming to America: A History of Immigration and Ethnicity in American Life* and Edwin Guillet's *The Great Migration: The Atlantic Crossing by Sailing-Ship Since 1770*. Also look for books specific to her ethnic background to learn about her culture.

City Directories

Most city directories were first published during the late nineteenth and early twentieth centuries; however, there are some dating as far back as the late 1700s. The more recent directories, however, may be more beneficial when researching women.

City directories generally list names of adults, including adult children living with parents. Some also list occupation, name of employer, home address and spouse's name. Although it is uncommon, I've found directories that list a date of death for some-

one in the household. More commonly, the spouse is listed as a widow or widower the year following the death. In small communities, directories may tell where a family relocated if they moved.

A helpful feature of some twentieth-century city directories is the *Householder's Index* or *Crisscross Directory*. It is sometimes found in the back of the directory, or it may be a totally separate volume. These are alphabetical/numerical listings of streets followed by house numbers and inhabitants instead of an alphabetical listing of individuals. The *Householder's Index* is a wonderful way to discover the names of your ancestors' neighbors.

Here are two examples of how city directories and the *Householder's Index* can aid in tracking women. I was looking for a woman who lived in Colorado Springs in the late 1970s. I found Mindy McFarland (not her real name) living at 53 Main Street in 1978. The next year, she was not listed. For a clue as to whether she moved or perhaps married, I turned to the *Householder's Index* for Main Street, number 53. The inhabitant, Joe Thayer, was living at that address with a wife named Mindy. I located a marriage record to confirm that I had the right person, then continued to follow her in the city directories to the present under her married name.

In another case, I was trying to determine whether Daisy Hunington (not her real name) was divorced or widowed. Colorado death records are difficult for someone other than a relative to obtain, so I consulted city directories to eliminate hours of searching through obituaries and divorce indexes. Daisy and Randy Hunington lived in the same house for three years after their marriage. In the fourth year, they were listed in separate households. Randy was listed apart from Daisy for several years, ruling out his death. The directory listings also narrowed down the time period in which to search for a divorce record.

There are many books about urban living that will add details when writing about women who lived in cities. Christine Stansell's *City of Women: Sex and Class in New York, 1789–1860* is one example.

Voter Lists and Registrations

As mentioned earlier, women were granted the right to vote when the Nineteenth Amendment passed in 1920, although some southern states did not ratify this amendment immediately. Prior to this time, however, some individual western states passed woman's suffrage in the mid- to late-1800s (see the Source Checklist in Appendix C for the dates when states passed women's voting laws). Where women were allowed to vote, you may want to check for surviving voter lists and registrations.

Of particular note on this topic is the state of New Jersey because of its early woman's suffrage. As of 1776, the state constitution defined voters as "all free inhabitants" who met the property and residency requirements, which neither disfranchised or enfranchised women. Many women voted in local elections as a result. In 1790 New Jersey formally adopted an election law that referred to its voters as "he or she."

One legislator stated that the New Jersey constitution gave the right to "maids or widows *black or white*." Unfortunately, in 1807, traditional attitudes forced a bill in that state that disfranchised both women and blacks.[11]

In the western states, in particular, it was common for women to be allowed to vote in school board elections and to be active themselves on school boards, so minutes of meetings as well as voter records can be beneficial.

For more information on woman's suffrage, see Susan B. Anthony's (and others) multivolume *The History of Woman Suffrage*, Mari Jo and Paul Buhle's *The Concise History of Woman Suffrage*, Edward Turner's "Women's Suffrage in New Jersey" in *Smith College Studies in History*, Henry Shinn's "An Early New Jersey Poll List," *Pennsylvania Magazine of History and Biography*, and others listed in the Bibliography. Also see chapter one, Legislative Petitions, and chapter five, Women's Rights and Moral Reform Movements.

Military Records and Pensions

Many women have served in the military throughout history—as nurses, spies, disguised as men, and as regular servicewomen in twentieth-century wars. Nearly twenty thousand women served as camp followers during the Revolutionary War as cooks, doctors, nurses, guides, seamstresses and laundresses. Some were paid; others volunteered to follow both British and American camps, aiding men. A few women even acquired rank and obtained pensions for their service.

During all wars, females participated by disguising themselves as men. It is estimated that four hundred to eight hundred women served in the Union and Confederate armies disguised as soldiers. (See books such as Richard Hall's *Patriots in Disguise: Women Warriors of the Civil War* and others in the Bibliography.) There were also camp followers during this war. For women who served in the military, consult Virginia Purdy and Robert Gruber's *American Women and the U.S. Armed Forces: A Guide to the Records of Military Agencies in the National Archives Relating to Women.* You are more likely, however, to find traditional women mentioned in pension records either created by their husbands or as widows and mothers of deceased veterans.

Ruth Kavanaugh was the former widow of Travis Booton who served on the Virginia Line in the Revolutionary War. She applied for a widow's pension on 6 August 1852 in Madison County, Kentucky.[12] Her pension application tells that she was eighty-four. She and Travis married about 1787 in Greenbriar County, Virginia, and they had one child, a daughter named Mary Ann who was now married to Joel Emory of Madison County, Kentucky. Travis died in April 1814, and Ruth married a second time to William Kavanaugh, who died in October 1829, leaving no heirs. The pension application also gives Ruth's maiden name: Estill. That's *a lot* of family information from one record. Widow's pensions are typically filled with this kind of data. Also, women tended to reference events of the war with what was happening in their personal lives, such as when a child was born. When applying for a widow's pension, women had to provide supporting documents to prove their marriage and birth of their children.

Loyalist women during the Revolution also made pension claims. Mary Beth Norton discusses these petitions in her article, "Eighteenth-Century American Women in Peace and War: The Case of the Loyalists," in a 1976 issue of the *William and Mary Quarterly.*

It was on a Civil War pension application of James H. Goforth of Dade County, Missouri, that I learned the maiden name of his wife Mary Ann—Davidson—and the date she married James. When James applied for his pension, he had to provide information on his wife and when and where he married her, as well as the names and birth dates of all of his children.[13]

In another Civil War pension application, Sarah Points of Pleasanton, Iowa, was the widowed mother of Andrew Points. She applied for a pension based on her son's service. The record recounts her son's military activities and when and where he died in battle. It also gives her present circumstances and why she was applying for the pension.[14]

Black women were also entitled to make widow's pension applications for their husbands' service in the Civil War. See chapter three, African American Women.

To locate pension records, you must look under the veteran's name. Again, this section only gives a condensed look at possible records relating to the military. For more information on pension applications, see *Guide to Genealogical Research in the National Archives* and James C. Neagles's *U.S. Military Records: A Guide to Federal and State Sources, Colonial America to the Present.*

Consider how a woman felt and coped while her husband was away serving the country. What additional duties and responsibilities did she acquire? Was she pregnant when he enlisted? How many children were at home to tend? Were there any children old enough to help her? Was she literate so that she could correspond with her husband, or would she have had a friend or relative write and read letters for her? When writing about women who stayed on the homefront or who served in the military, consult books such as Mary Beth Norton's *Liberty's Daughters: The Revolutionary Experience of American Women, 1750–1800,* L.P. Brockett and Mary C. Vaughan's *Women at War: A Record of Their Patriotic Contributions, Heroism, Toils, and Sacrifice During the Civil War* and others listed in the Bibliography.

Orphan's and Guardianship Records

When a woman was left a widow with minor children, the children were considered orphans in need of a legal guardian. The guardian was almost always a male relative who would ensure the child's welfare until reaching majority. Even fathers of motherless children sometimes sought guardianships, usually because his children were entitled to an inheritance from the mother's family. There are also cases where both par-

ents were living, but a guardian was appointed to protect an inheritance from another relative, such as a grandparent. Many guardianships were recorded, often in probate court minutes if the loose papers have been destroyed. Regardless, they are worth seeking if they do exist.

According to *Black's Law Dictionary,* a helpful reference when researching court records, there are many different types of guardians. For example, a testamentary guardian is one that is appointed in the will of a child's parent. A guardian by election is one that the minor child chooses. A guardian *ad litem,* usually an attorney, is one appointed by the court to represent the minor child in a legal dispute or an adoption. In one case in Gallia County, Ohio, both parents were still living when a guardian *ad litem* was appointed. William Donnally conveyed his land about 1840 to his children to avoid the land being seized and sold to pay his debts. Two of his children were of age, the other eight were minors. Donnally's children were eventually sued, and a guardian *ad litem* was appointed to represent the minor children.[15]

Land Records

Probably some of the earliest records you will find in existence are land records. Even when courthouses burned, many deeds were rerecorded since land ownership was not something people wanted to dispute. Since married women were "covered" by their husbands (*femes covert*), they could not legally engage in contracts or land transactions without their husbands' approval. Early land dealings may give you only the husband's name with either no mention of a wife or just her first name. If the woman were widowed, divorced or single (*feme sole*), however, you may find her transacting her own land sales. As men and women moved west to take advantage of the Homestead Act of 1862, many *femes sole* purchased land under this act.

One area to watch for is when a man, or a husband and wife, sold property to a woman or a husband and wife for a dollar or some other small consideration. The sellers or grantors are likely the woman's parents or other close relatives. In a deed recorded in 1849, Isaac Baker and his wife, Rachel, sold to Elizabeth A. Snyder two acres of land for one dollar. Look also at the land description:

> [Land in] the town of Winchester [Frederick County, Virginia] containing two acres more or less being part of a larger lot owned by John Baker dec'd which larger lot is bounded as follows on the North by the lands of Geo W Baker on the West by the lands of the late Hannah Dunbar on the South by the road leading from Winchester to Berryville and on the East by the lands of the said John Baker dec'd the portion hereby conveyed was conveyed by said John Baker to said Isaac Baker by deed dated April 29 1840 and duly recorded in said county and mentioned by said John Baker in his will now of record in said county, at the West end of said larger lot. . . .[16]

With the land "being part of a larger lot owned by John Baker," one that is bounded on the north by the lands of George W. Baker, and that contains land conveyed to Isaac Baker from John Baker as mentioned in John's will, what do you think the chances are that Elizabeth A. Snyder's maiden name is Baker? Pretty good.

You may notice that when the man is buying property, no wife is named or mentioned. But when it comes time to sell the property, you may find a release of her dower rights (see Appendix A on women's legal rights). Some colonies, such as Virginia, had dower releases early in their history; some colonies, such as Connecticut, and later, states, were slower to incorporate dower releases in their deeds, if they ever did at all. A wife's right of dower meant that she was entitled upon widowhood to a one-third life interest in her husband's property. On occasion, a wife may have refused to release her dower, or it was inadvertently overlooked. If she did not release her dower, she could still make a claim to the property after her husband died. A release of dower may happen several years later when it became necessary to clear the title. For reasons unknown, Malissa Hamilton of Macon County, Missouri, for example, did not release her dower until three years after her husband sold a parcel of land to Stephan Scott on 4 May 1840.[17]

Some deeds offer only clues such as the Baker/Snyder deed above, others give little additional information about the woman than you already know, and others may give you wonderful details, such as the opening paragraph in this Knox County, Ohio, deed of 1848: "Know all men by these presents, that we Ann Losh formerly Ann Wadell, now wife of Adam Losh of the County of Knox . . ."[18]

Finally, look at all the relationships stated in the beginning of this deed from Nicholas County, Kentucky:

> Know all men by these presents that we Henry McClintock and Catherine McClintock wife of the said Henry (which Catherine was formerly Catherine Johnson and daughter of Ann Johnson, who is now deceased and who was one of the heirs at law of John Harding decd. who died in Nicholas County in the state of Kentucky about two years ago more or less) and Mary Harding widow of Charles Harding deceased which Charles Harding was the son and one of the heirs at law of the aforesaid John Harding of Kentucky . . . And I the said Mary Harding being the natural guardian of my two infant children, Henry Harding and Jane Harding, who are the children and heirs at law of my said decd. husband . . .[19]

As mentioned, you just never know what a record will tell you. *Check everything.* An indispensable guide once you get involved in researching land records is Marylynn Salmon's *Women and the Law of Property in Early America.* This will also supplement your research when writing a narrative. Other social histories on female land ownership are Nancy Osterud's *Bonds of Community: The Lives of Farm Women in Nineteenth-Century New York* and Julie Jones-Eddy's *Homesteading Women: An Oral History of Colorado, 1890–1950.*

Marriage Records

In some states, no license was required for a couple to be married. For those states requiring licenses, keep in mind that some couples took out a license or application but never made it to the altar, so you need to also check for a record of the marriage taking place. Marriage bonds were posted in some states to help offset costs of legal action in case the marriage was nullified. The groom and either the father or brother of the bride posted a bond; if a woman posted bond, it may be the bride's mother because the father was deceased. In the case of Jesse Curry and Mary Strader of Green County, Kentucky, a bond was posted on 9 December 1839 by Richard Strader, probably Mary's father, but possibly her brother or uncle.[20]

Where there are surviving marriage licenses, you may find a wealth of information on both the bride and groom, and it may also give their mothers' maiden names, as this example of an 1860 license from Madison County, Virginia, shows:

> Date of Marriage: November 27th 1860
> Place of Marriage: at the residence of
> B.F.T. Conway, Madison County
> Full Names of Parties Married: Catlett
> Conway Fitzhugh and Ellen
> Sommerville Conway

Age of Husband: Twenty-nine years

Age of Wife: Twenty-two years

Condition of Husband (widowed or single): Single

Condition of Wife (widowed or single): Single

Place of Husband's Birth: King George County, Virginia

Place of Wife's Birth: Madison County, Virginia

Place of Husband's Residence: Richmond City

Place of Wife's Residence: Madison County, Virginia

Name of Husband's Parents: James M. Fitzhugh and Mary F. Stuart

Name of Wife's Parents: Battaile F.T. Conway and Mary A. Wallace

Occupation of Husband: Merchant

Signed by Catlett C. Fitzhugh 10 November 1860

The marriage was performed on the date specified above.[21]

Be cautious when dealing with colonial marriage records. You may find a man marrying a *Mrs*. Mary Smith. This does not necessarily mean that she was married previously. The term *Mrs*., which is originally an abbreviation for *Mistress*, was used for both married and unmarried women and girls. It denoted a social position.

Consider how your female ancestor would have met and married her husband. Was he older than she? By how many years? Was he someone she had known for a long time? Was he a distant cousin? What were their expected roles in marriage? How did husbands and wives treat each other? To learn more about marriage and courtship customs to combine with your genealogical records when writing a narrative, see books such as Ellen K. Rothman's *Hands and Hearts: A History of Courtship in America*, Helen Fisher's *Anatomy of Love: The Natural History of Monogamy, Adultery, and Divorce*, John D'Emilio and Estelle B. Freedman's *Intimate Matters: A History of Sexuality in America* and others listed in the Bibliography.

Medical Records

For the most part, medical records may be difficult to obtain. This is because medical records do not fall under governmental jurisdiction, but private jurisdiction, where the records could be destroyed at any time or withheld from the public. There are some record collections that are open to the public, however. Most noteworthy are two collections that have been microfilmed and are available at the Family History Library in Salt Lake City, Utah, or through rental from one of its worldwide family history centers.

The Eugenics Record Office

The Eugenics Record Office (ERO) was in operation between 1910 and 1944. According to an article published by Thomas H. Roderick et al. in the June 1994 *National Genealogical Society Quarterly* about the collection, the ERO's purpose "was to study human genetics and to use this knowledge to reduce heritable problems in the human species." Over the thirty-four-year period, genetic and genealogical data to determine human traits was compiled from thousands of individuals. Field workers gathered information from patients in mental institutions and from their families. Forms were sent to interested college teachers around the country to use as part of class projects. Data were also gathered from volunteers who had special hereditary defects. In sum, there are about forty thousand pedigrees on file. There is an index to the files by surname, locality and trait.

Some of the genealogies on file take researchers back to the early and middle 1800s. Information contained in these records includes name or full maiden name, birthplace and birth date, date and place of marriage, total number of sons and daughters, diseases and illnesses, surgical operations, cause of death and age at death, height and weight, color of hair and eyes, complexion of skin color and more. Much of the information is documented and includes data from individuals who had personal knowledge of many of the events that are recorded.

The locations of the institutions and families the field workers visited span nineteen states: Arkansas, California, Connecticut, Illinois, Indiana, Maine, Maryland, Massachusetts, Michigan, New Jersey, North Carolina, Ohio, Pennsylvania, South Carolina, Texas, Utah, Virginia, West Virginia and Wisconsin. Those forms filled out by college students came from even more states.

This massive genealogical medical-record collection is on 520 rolls of microfilm. To access the series in the Family History Library Catalog, look for the following headings:

United States—Medical Records—Eugenics. Or look up one of the states mentioned above, followed by Medical Records.

Here is one example of the wealth of data found in these records:

1. *Genealogical Data [of Mary Knox]*
   Mary Elizabeth (Thomas) Knox
   born 23 Dec 1883, Hotchkissville, Conn.
   Married 18 Jan 1902 to William Austin Knox, son of George Knox born in Hotchkissville, and Dolly Hendrickson, born Southington

   Father: Frederick Alvin Thomas, born in High Plains
   Father's father: Ryan Alvin Thomas
   Father's mother: Mary Elizabeth Newton

   Mother: Charlotte Hall, born in Hotchkissville in 1856
   Mother's father: John Thomas Hall
   Mother's mother: Harriet Esther Smith

   Children (all born in Hotchkissville):
   George b. 17 June 1902
   Mildred b. 6 Aug 1904
   Erwin b. 1 Feb 1906
   Wilfred b. 18 Jan 1911
   Clarence b. 9 July 1912

2. *Physical and Mental Data [of Mary Knox]*
   Memory: very poor
   Mathemat. Capac.: couldn't do arith. at all

Ability in singing: none

Ability in instr. music: none

Ability in drawing or coloring: none

Ability in oratory: used to speak pieces, but didn't care for it.

Predilection for reading: says she likes to read, but doesn't at all because of the ch[ildren]; doesn't like sewing

House is untidy, ill-kept in extreme—children are dirty and "wild"—little or no discipline

Temperament: nervous

Other marked Mental Traits: Winter 1910–1911 they wished to send her to Middletown Insane Hosp—she heard voices—confused—insight, however, for she knew the voices were false

Other marked Physical Traits: says she is more or less nervous—with frequent psychosis—when pregnant.

Diseases to which Liable: Used to have headache in forehead just above eyes age 14–20

Grave Illnesses: Fallen uterus.

Surgical Operations: no

3. Biographical Data [of Mary Knox]

Residences Year and Place: Hotchkissville—Lived in Reynolds Bridge from May 1911–Jan 1912

School Education: Began sch. age 7 yrs. in Hotchkissville village sch—attended there until age 14—Then attended Academy a

time—Then in 7th grade in Mitchell sch until age 17.

Other Training: none—never worked out at housework

Studies for which there was strong preference: "I was stupid and slow in sch—especially arith."

From age 4 yrs lived with her paternal grandmother in Hotchkissville and also after mar[riage]. For 9 yrs she and husb[and] (Mr. Knox) lived with this grandmother. Her mother when Mary was but 4 yrs of age was committed to Middletown Insane Hospital and tho she was allowed to return home later she was not considered able to care for Mary.

4. Social Data [of Mary Knox]

Religious Interests, Denomination: Confirmed in Episcopal. Church Member? Yes

Name of Local Church attended: St. Paul's. Doesn't attend.[22]

If you discover a family member in the ERO, you may also want to read historical accounts of the eugenics movement, which had controversial ramifications.

Northwestern Memorial Hospital

Another group of documents at the Family History Library in Salt Lake City, Utah, is from Chicago's Northwestern Memorial Hospital records, 1896–1933 (FHL microfilm numbers 1315895–905). These records document births, abortions and miscarriages for thousands of women who lived in the area, primarily immigrant women. Information varies from year to year. The earlier records give the woman's married name, street address, number of living children the woman has delivered ("para"), number born at term, ethnicity (many records were for Russian Jews, some Irish Catholics, Polish Catholics, American Protestants, etc.), referral person or agency ("thro former patient," "thro Hull House," etc.), the woman's condition (e.g., "urgent, threatened abortion in 3rd month"), case number, confinement date. Later records provide the woman's full married name, date, address, nationality, by whom sent, para, number at term, when to expect confinement, whether labors were normal, attended by (physician and student), date, diagnosis, case or confinement number.

The most recent records also give information commonly found on birth certificates, such as the wife's maiden name, the husband's name, places of birth for husband and wife, the weight of the baby and the baby's name. The records are grouped by year; unfortunately, they are not indexed. But if you have an ancestor who lived in Chicago between 1896 and 1933 near Northwestern Hospital, and especially if she was a Russian Jew or an immigrant who lived in a nearby tenement, it may be well worth your time to do a page-by-page search.

Here are a few entries from the application books, where women applied to be seen at the hospital:

> Mrs. Abram Berman
> lives near Canal St.
> para iv, 3 at term

> [currently] in third month [of pregnancy]
> Russian Jewess
> [condition:] Threatened abortion in third month
> [referral:] thro [sic] former patient
> Case 169—Inevitable abortion Mch 28th 1897

> Mary Rudolph Salaterski
> June 1, [1932]
> 1474 W. Huron 3rd floor
> Polish Catholic
> para iii 2 at term expects confinement Aug 29, 1932
> labors [of previous delivery] normal: 2 (1 [birth by] midwife)
> attended by Dr. Bradenman student Bruder 8-19-1932
> Diagnosis: . . . male 9 [lbs.] case or confinement #327
> Mother's birthplace: Ill. Age 25
>   Maiden name: Smolen
> Father's birthplace: Poland Age 35
>   Baby's name: Rudolph Jr.[23]

Doctors' and Midwives' Journals

Another type of medical record to search for is midwives' or doctors' journals that may have been microfilmed or published. In New York City alone, five hundred midwives were practicing in 1906. Other urban areas, such as Chicago and Boston, had large numbers of midwives. Many immigrant women felt more comfortable with a midwife than a male doctor because this is what they were used to in their homelands. As discussed in chapter one, surviving midwives' journals may have been published or you may be able to locate them as a manuscript collection in a library or other repository. These contain entries for births, abortions or miscarriages the midwife attended. Check the *National Union Catalog of Manuscript Collections*. (Also see chapter five, Sexuality.)

Childbirth, birth control and abortion are covered in various social histories, as well. See John D'Emilio and Estelle B. Freeman's *Intimate Matters: A History of Sexuality in America*, Linda Gordon's *Woman's Body, Woman's Right: A Social History of Birth Control in America*, and Richard and Dorothy Wertz's *Lying-In: A History of Childbirth in America*.

Tuberculin Sanatoriums

Don't overlook medical institutions such as tuberculin sanatoriums. Tuberculosis, also known as consumption, claimed many lives in the late nineteenth and early twentieth centuries. Those who contracted the disease may have spent time in one of the tuberculin sanatoriums around the country. Philip P. Jacobs's *The Campaign Against Tuberculosis in the United States, Including a Directory of Institutions Dealing With Tuberculosis in the United States and Canada* would be a good starting place if there is a family story of one of your women ancestors contracting the disease. Lulu Jarrett (not her real name), who died at the age of twenty-four in 1913 from pulmonary tuberculosis, spent time in Nordrach Ranch Sanatorium in Colorado Springs. Tracking down the records was a challenge. A local history librarian remembered that many of the records for the

Nordrach Ranch were kept in a university professor's garage. In the library, there was also an abundance of magazine and newspaper articles on the sanatorium that, although not publishing patients' names, gave excellent information on the daily care and treatment of tuberculin patients. Another book on this disease is Sheila Rothman's *Living in the Shadow of Death: Tuberculosis and the Social Experience of Illness in American History*.

Insane Asylums

Many women throughout the history of our country have been committed to insane asylums; a good number of them were totally sane. There have been husbands who wanted to "get rid" of their wives for various reasons and found commitment a viable solution. A husband may have wanted a divorce to marry someone else, and his wife's insanity was legal grounds in some states. A husband might seek total control of his wife's property, but because he couldn't sell the land without his wife releasing her dower, he found a way to have her declared insane and incompetent. Some men committed their wives simply for being outspoken. This was the case of Elizabeth Parsons Ware Packard, who defended religious opinions that conflicted with her church. At the direction of her husband, she was literally kidnapped in June 1860, examined by two doctors her husband hired, then declared insane. She was kept in the Illinois State Hospital for the Insane for three years. A portion of her memoirs and those of other women committed to insane asylums have been published in Jeffrey Geller and Maxine Harris's *Women of the Asylum: Voices From Behind the Walls, 1840–1945.*[24]

As mentioned earlier, many women were committed for ailments that today would be labeled postpartum blues, menopause, and manic depression or bipolar disease. Some were schizophrenic or had other mental disorders. On the federal censuses for 1840, 1850, 1860, 1870 and 1880, look carefully in the column that denotes insane persons. On the 1880 schedule that lists Nancy Bane and her family in Gallia County, Ohio, the "tick" or "hash" mark in the insane column is barely readable; one might easily overlook it as a smudge or speck of dust on the microfilm.[25] A further examination into the 1880 Schedule for the Defective, Dependent, and Delinquent Classes revealed that Nancy had been a patient at the Central Ohio Institution and had twenty-four attacks of mania. Her attacks began at age forty-seven. She was kept in a cell and discharged from the institution in 1868.[26]

If you find a woman in an insane asylum, consider what her life would have been like while in the institution. What about when she was released? How would her family and friends have treated her?

Also look at court records for commitment papers. Sally Treadwell was committed in 1908 by her husband:

To the Honorable Probate Court:
    The undersigned, a Selectman of the town of Greenwich, hereby re-

ports that pursuant to the order of said Court, passed on this 20th day of May, A.D., 1908, he has fully investigated the facts in the case of said Sally Treadwell represented to be insane and an indigent person not a pauper, and is of the opinion that said Sally Treadwell is a pauper, within the meaning of chapter 196, of the public acts, of this State and further reports that he finds the said Sally Treadwell to be possessed of no property, real and personal as far as he can ascertain. That he finds that said Sally Treadwell is married and mother of Two children. That her husband is a Coachman and is not possessed of any real or personal Estate and that his pay is no more than sufficient to care for the children. . . . She has lived in furnished rooms with her children. Her husband [is] living with his employer. . . .

The undersigned S. Bolton, physician hereby reports that pursuant to an order of said Court passed on the 20 day of May, 1908, he has fully investigated the facts in the case of Sally Treadwell represented to be insane, and is of the opinion that said Sally Treadwell is insane. . . .

He has formed the above opinion regarding Sally Treadwell from (a) the conduct and conversation observed by him personally, and from (b) other facts ascertained, including those communicated to him by others, which are as follows:

(a) Conduct, attitude, conversation, etc. observed by him personally: Delusion of persecution.

(b) Other facts indicative of insanity, including those communicated to him by others: Having a large number of children by different men of influence. . . . Ten children during two years [sic]. Many wealthy people quoted as being fathers during this time. . . .

It is therefore ordered, that the said Sally Treadwell be taken . . . without delay to the Connecticut Hospital for the Insane . . . where she shall be kept and supported so long as may be requisite.[27]

I then found Sally on the 1910 census in the Connecticut Hospital for the Insane:

Treadwell, Sally, boarder, female, black, age 26, married once, married five years, two children born, two children living, Sally was born in Georgia, both parents born in Georgia, able to read and write.[28]

Wines's *Report on the Defective, Dependent, and Delinquent Classes,* cited earlier, gives the location in each state of all the insane asylums in operation at the time. With this information, write a letter to the historical society in the city where the asylum existed, and ask if someone knows where the records are currently housed.

If you find a woman who's been committed by her husband but does not return to live with him, another document to seek is a divorce record.

Divorce Records

In the colonial and early national periods, there were two types of divorce: divorce *a vinculo matrimonii,* which meant an absolute divorce with the right for both parties to remarry, and divorce *a mensa et thoro,* or separation from bed and board, meaning neither party could remarry. Some southern colonies did not allow divorces at all; others would grant only a divorce *a mensa et thoro.* Grounds for divorce, such as desertion, cruelty, adultery, homosexuality or bigamy, varied from one colony (and later, states) to the next, with divorce laws and practices evolving over time.[29] (See Appendix A regarding women's legal status.)

Until the mid-1800s, divorces were legislative actions in many colonies and states. Some states had dual jurisdiction: both state legislatures and chancery courts heard divorce cases. Virginia, for example, had a dual system of legislative and judicial divorce until 1850. Legislative divorce was active until 1897 in Delaware, the last state to change over to judicial jurisdiction. When more and more cases came before the legislature, local courts (e.g., circuit courts) began taking on the petitions since jurists believed that the local court could more aptly determine the charges and make a judgment.[30]

In our nation's early history, more men than women filed for divorce; however, after the Revolution, women petitioners outnumbered men. Divorce petitions increased significantly after the Civil War: between 1867 and 1871, there were 53,574 divorces granted in this country; between 1877 and 1881, the figure rose to 89,284. During the mid-nineteenth century, a few states, such as Indiana, were reputed as divorce mills, having easy divorce laws and short residency requirements. This made "migratory" divorce quite popular. If a person was living in a state with strict divorce laws, he or she might establish residency in a more lenient state. In Indiana, besides fulfilling the short residency requirement, the petitioner only needed to place an ad in a newspaper where the action was filed; otherwise, the spouse was not notified until after the decree. And in Indiana, divorces were irrevocable.[31] Also it may benefit you to check the divorce laws of those states nearest to where your ancestors lived, in case of a migratory divorce.

As mentioned earlier, not all petitions resulted in divorce decrees; sometimes the ratio was as high as two unsuccessful petitions for every divorce granted.[32] Even if your female ancestor never petitioned for divorce, perhaps her friend or neighbor did, with your ancestor serving as a witness and giving a testimony.

Men sometimes placed public notices in newspapers repudiating their wives' debts, such as the one described in an 1870s newspaper article:

Samuel Goodman (not his real name), who lives somewhere in the neighborhood of————, and whose nature, we fear, is far from befitting his name, advertises in our columns that he will not be responsible for any of his wife's debts, she having left his bed and board. Mrs. Goodman alleges that she had too much reason for her departure, having made complaint before Justice Bergen, on Tuesday last, that her husband was in the habit of thrashing her instead of cherishing her. The case was dismissed, on account of an informality in the complaint, and Goodman was set at liberty.

You may also find public advertisements in newspapers for runaway wives and ads placed by couples stating they are separating.

Divorce records are not only fascinating, but can reveal quite a bit of information on women ancestors:

Isaac D. Pounds v. Charlotte F. Pounds. April 1, 1851: married at Columbus on May 5, 1841 to Charlotte F. Tupper; he left for California on Feb. 19, 1849, intending to return in about eighteen months; he had previously moved his wife and three children to Loudenville in Richland County where his mother resides and left them there with abundant means of support; he arrived back in Columbus on Oct. 10, 1850 and found that Charlotte had moved back here; adultery; she abandoned the children and residence in Columbus in a state of pregnancy and went to parts unknown shortly before his arrival; the children he found scattered among different families. Granted divorce and custody, June 2, 1851.[33]

An early divorce record from Hanover County, Virginia, of 1798, gives a wealth of information on a woman. Peter Bowles married Sally Parker on 8 February 1798. On 28 April 1798 Sally delivered a child. Peter knew it wasn't his, and "his unfortunate and culpable wife, has since sworn [it] was the child of Hartwell Boatright." Although Sally was "nearly seven months advanced in pregnancy on the day of their marriage, she cautiously avoided making a discovery of her situation, and suffered your petitioner to remain totally ignorant of the melancholy misfortune which she was with premeditation about to bring upon him." Peter felt that it was impossible to live with Sally in happiness together. Sally consented to the divorce, and it was granted on 17 July 1798.[34]

Sarah Cope petitioned for a divorce from her husband in 1772 in Fairfield County, Connecticut. The petition begins by giving her maiden name, Sarah Wheeler. Sarah claimed that her husband John had "during the last Winter and since said Marriage went [on] a Voyage to the West Indies, and while he was there he lived a loose, vicious, scandalous, and lewd incontinent Life and had carnal Knowledge there of the Bodies of certain lewd Women and thereby contracted and caught the foul Distemper commonly called the French Pox . . . and hath communicated the same to the [Petitioner]. . . ."[35] Unfortunately, the rest of

the record either didn't survive or wasn't microfilmed, so we will never know if Sarah was granted her divorce.

In this area, too, consider how a woman's life changed as a result of obtaining a divorce. Or how it did or did not change if the divorce was not granted. If she was granted a divorce, how did she support herself? Did she marry again? A divorce also affected her legal and social status. A good social history of divorce to supplement these records when writing a woman's biography is Glenda Riley's *Divorce: An American Tradition*.

Wills and Probate

The wills of fathers and husbands are important documents in tracing women. There isn't a genealogist in the world who doesn't look for a will hoping it will state, "I leave to my daughter Anne, wife of Samuel Harris," which gives you a solid connection to a woman's father and her husband. On rare occasions a husband will name his wife and give her maiden name in a will, stating, "my beloved wife, Mary, formerly Mary Rogers." More likely, you will find wills that just say, "my beloved wife, Sophia," or simply, "my wife." After all, everyone knew who his wife was; there was no need to name her. Similarly, if you see "my now wife" in a man's will, it referred to the woman to whom he was married when he made out the will—not that he necessarily had been married before. Relationships stated in wills may require further research. In William S. Davidson's 1857 will from Dade County, Missouri, he named his sons-in-law James H. Goforth and Lemuel L. Carlock. William did not name his daughters, though. By seeking other records, such as marriages or censuses, we would learn the names of the women who married Goforth and Carlock: William's daughters, Mary Ann and Angelina.[36] Always check for the probate packet. If still extant, this file may contain papers for each step in the probate process: inventory, estate distribution, whereabouts of heirs, etc.

As mentioned under Cemetery Records, you will want to consider how your female ancestor's life changed once she became a widow. Her husband's death affected her legal status. How did her husband provide for her if he left a will? If he died intestate, what was she entitled to inherit? For social histories on inheritance customs to help augment your woman's biography, see David Hackett Fischer's *Albion's Seed: Four British Folkways in America* and Carole Shammas, Marylynn Salmon and Michel Dahlin's *Inheritance in America: From Colonial Times to the Present.*

Court Records

Colonial court records hold fascinating facts on women ancestors. You may find women accused of such crimes as witchcraft, scolding husbands, gossiping about neighbors, being disrespectful to ministers and refusing to go to church. In August 1682, widow Mary Hamond was admonished for frequently absenting herself from the public ordinances. She was also admonished and ordered to pay witness fees to Thomas Day "for speaking reproachful words against the

worship of God in saying that going to hear the minister preach is the way to hell."[37]

If you've ever looked at colonial court records or read colonial histories, you are aware of the many citations of women who were presented for fornication and ordered to be whipped or pay a fine. Ever wonder why couples, such as William and Naomy Seargent of Essex County, Massachusetts, would willingly admit to the court that they engaged in premarital sex?[38] One reason may have been because some New England churches would not baptize a child who was born less than seven months after the marriage unless the couple publicly confessed their sin. In some church records you may find a notation of "C.F." after a baptism entry. This meant "Confessed to Fornication." Katharine P. Randall wrote an excellent article on "Those Early Firstborns of Eighteenth-Century America: Moral Lapses or Planned Parenthood?" for the April 1984 *New York Genealogical and Biographical Record*, going into more detail on this subject.

Another interesting type of court record involves bastardy cases (see chapter five, Bastardy and Infanticide). Illegitimate children were a financial burden on the community, so officials often tried to coerce a mother to name the father of her child. When an unmarried woman went into labor, the midwife would question her about paternity since it was believed that during the "time of her travell [travail]" the mother would be incapable of lying about the father's identity. Punishment was meted out to both parties for fornication before marriage. By the mid-1700s, however, the courts let churches hand out punishment, while the courts concentrated on getting financial support for the child.[39] One aspect you should consider when you find a bastardy case is that there may be instances of false paternity accusations. One woman wrote to her illicit lover: "der loue [love] . . . I am a child by you and I will ether kil it or lay it to an other. . . . I have had many children and none [of the fathers] have none of them [to support]."[40]

Another area affected by the presence of illegitimate children is inheritance. Inheritance laws varied from state to state and evolved over time. A good starting place, however, to learn more about this topic is Shammas, Salmon and Dahlin's *Inheritance in America: From Colonial Times to the Present*. For more information on the colonial era's crimes and punishments, see works such as George Dow's *Every Day Life in the Massachusetts Bay Colony* and D'Emilio and Freedman's *Intimate Matters: A History of Sexuality in America*.

School Records

Most girls in rural communities attended one-room schoolhouses at some time in their lives. While education for girls was not a big priority to many farming families, after the Revolution, young girls usually attended school for a few years. It was more common for middle- and upper-class girls to attend boarding schools. These academies were usually located in small towns and drew students from around the country.

Most of a woman's education through the middle of the nineteenth century primarily consisted of domestic and "womanly" skills: sewing, needlework, painting, singing, dancing, playing the harpsichord or piano. As women's seminaries and colleges opened, the educational emphasis was on thinking and reasoning. Seminaries and colleges for women had their start in the late eighteenth century, with two Young Ladies Academies opening: one in 1787 in Philadelphia and one in 1797 in Boston. Several other seminaries followed and opened around the country. By 1800, forty thousand women were enrolled in seminaries and colleges. In 1833, Oberlin College in Ohio was the first to offer equal education to men and women of all races. (See the Source Checklist in Appendix C for a listing of higher education schools that accepted women.)

After the Revolution, many women went to college or normal schools and became teachers. "Two historians have estimated that fully 25 percent of native-born female New Englanders alive in the antebellum years taught school at some time during their lives."[41] Between 1870 and 1890 the number of female teachers jumped from 90,000 to 250,000.[42] (See chapter five, Women's Work.)

For school records, if the institution still exists, write directly to it. If it does not, try writing to the local historical society to see where the records might be stored. For information on teachers, start by writing to the school district where the school was located to see if they still have employment records. The social histories on teaching and education will also provide you with information to write your narrative; in particular, see Barbara J. Finkelstein's "Schooling and Schoolteachers: Selected Bibliography of Autobiographies in the Nineteenth Century" in volume 14 of *History of Education Quarterly,* Polly Kaufman's *Women Teachers on the Frontier* and Barbara Solomon's *In the Company of Educated Women: A History of Women and Higher Education in America.*

As you can see, it doesn't matter in which time period your female ancestors lived; there are many sources available for researching them. If you haven't begun researching in any of these records, there is more information on the common sources in basic genealogical guidebooks. Remember, also, that the Source Checklist in Appendix C is there to help remind you of possible records to seek. Review this list as you research each female ancestor.

CHAPTER THREE

Additional Sources for Ethnic Women

They are our countrywomen—they are our sisters, and to us as women, they have a right to look for sympathy with their sorrows, and effort and prayer for their rescue. . . .

Sarah and Angelina Grimke,
as quoted in Sara Evans's
Born for Liberty

Most of the records discussed in the previous chapter also encompass women of ethnic ancestry. If you are following the "rule" of genealogical research by starting with living generations and working backward in time, you will find women of all nationalities among vital records, censuses, cemetery records and so forth. Oral history, in particular, is an extremely important source for researching ethnic women. Stories of slavery, Native American removals, Holocaust internment, and immigration, for example, can lead you to many records. Some sources and methodologies specific to certain ethnic groups deserve mention, however.

Though it is beyond the scope of this book to discuss research on every ethnic group that your female heritage may entail, many excellent guidebooks deal with re-

searching specific ethnic origins. Check genealogical library catalogs or genealogical publishers' catalogs for these works. There are also social histories (see discussion in chapter five and the Bibliography) on specific ethnic backgrounds that will give you more information about your heritage.

African American Women

The number of black women kept in bondage over the years is staggering:[1]

- 1820—of 870,860 black women in America, 750,010 were slaves
- 1830—of 1,162,366 black women, 996,200 were slaves
- 1840—of 1,440,600 black women, 1,240,938 were slaves
- 1850—of 1,827,550 black women, 1,601,799 were slaves
- 1860—of 2,225,086 black women, 1,971,135 were slaves

During the Revolutionary War, the British commanders offered freedom to southern black slaves who would flee their masters' plantations. There were no age or sex restrictions, so many men and women took their children and fled. When the British left an American port, "they carried large numbers of former slaves away with them, approximately ten thousand from Savannah and Charleston alone." British commander Sir Guy Carleton ordered an enumeration of all blacks who sought the army's protection. In the process, the army obtained crude biographical details of the former slaves to determine whether they would be allowed to leave with the troops for England and Nova Scotia. "Blacks who had belonged to loyalists were excluded from the promise of freedom offered by the British during the war, as were any who had joined the British after November 1782," so these runaways were returned to their masters. All others were liberated.[2] For more information on blacks during the Revolution, see Mary Beth Norton's "The Fate of Some Black Loyalists of the American Revolution" in a 1973 issue of the *Journal of Negro History* and Benjamin Quarles's *The Negro in the American Revolution.* Some of the surviving embarkation lists and records may be found among the papers of the Continental Congress in the National Archives, microfilms M247, reel 66, item 53, 276–94; and M332, reel 7.[3]

While free blacks before emancipation are likely recorded by name in traditional records such as censuses, population schedules usually do not list the names of slaves. On the 1850 and 1860 special slave schedules, only the slave owner's name is given; each slave is enumerated by color (black or mulatto), sex and age. Thus it is important to know the name of the slave owner, which may be passed down through the generations in oral history. If, however, you have an ancestor, either free or slave, who died during the census year of 1850 or 1860

(1 June through 31 May in 1849–50 or 1859–60), the mortality schedule recorded the names of blacks and mulattoes who died during that year. These names, however, may not be included in many of the general indexes to these enumerations.

More likely, you will find records of slaves in deeds and wills by which they were sold or transferred to other people. Here is an example from Townsend Dade's will of 1761 in Stafford County, Virginia:[4]

> . . . I give to my daughter Elizabeth Washington, Dinah, Virgin, and their increase which she has in her possession. . . . I give to my grandson Langhorn Dade one negro man named Juba. . . . I give to my son Baldwin Dade, two negro men called Solomon and George. . . . I give to Sarah Dade widow of Cadwallador Dade two negroes Ben and Sukey. . . . I give to my daughter Frances Stuart the following negroes: Tom, Kate, Nancy, and their increase which she has in her possession. . . . I give to my son Horatio Dade the following negroes: Harry, Jolly, Daniel, Moses, and Nan and her increase. . . .

Some testators, upon their deaths, gave slaves their freedom:

> . . . This second day of May in the year of our Lord, One Thousand Seven Hundred and Eighty Three, I Derrick Kroesen . . . do make and ordain this my last Will and Testament. . . .

Item: It is my will that after my decease that my Negro woman Jude shall be set free and I give her her bed and the furniture thereto belonging all her wearing apperl [sic] and all her household furniture and the spinning wheel all to be her own property. My will further is in case she should by sickness be rendered uncapable [sic] of maintaining herself then it is my will that she shall be maintained by my three children. . . .

Item: It is my will that my Negro man Striffin, after my decease, he paying the sum of fifty pounds lawful money, he likewise shall be free and it is my will that my Negro girl Liddy, after my decease, she paying the sum of thirty pounds lawful money, she shall likewise be free with all her waring apperl [sic]. . . .

Codicil: April 30th, 1784, I, Derrick Kroesen in the Township of Southampton and County of Bucks and State of Pennsylvania. . . . It is also my will that after my decease my son Henry shall give to my Negro woman Jude four bushels of wheat every year and if she thinks proper to live in the kitchen during her life I give her that privilege. It is my will that my Negro man Striffin shall have three years time to pay the fifty pounds in, the first year after decease he shall pay fifteen pounds and the second year he shall pay fifteen pounds and the third year twenty pounds and likewise my Negro girl Lydia shall pay ten pounds yearly till the thirty pounds is paid. . . .[5]

It is interesting that Derrick Kroesen, a widower, makes Striffin and Lydia buy their freedom. Jude not only gets immediate freedom, household items, bushels of wheat and a place to live, but Derrick's children must take care of her if she becomes ill and cannot take care of herself. One can only speculate as to why this slave woman received such special treatment.

Deeds and wills that list unusual first names of slaves, such as Truelove, Tulip and Travers, may be helpful in tracing their whereabouts after the Civil War. Despite what you may have heard, slaves did not always take the surnames of their masters. Thus, looking at the 1870 census for slaves by their first names in the areas in which they lived during and prior to the war may be beneficial.

From the division of her father's estate, James Madison and Mary (Stuart) Fitzhugh are known to have inherited three slaves: Travers, Dick and Mary.[6] These slaves came into the household in 1831, so there may be a chance that some of them were still alive for the 1870 census, assuming they weren't sold and still lived with the Fitzhughs for the years between 1831 and 1870. Though a study of the widow Mary Fitzhugh's neighborhood in 1870 did reveal that her surrounding neighbors were black families, only one Mary appears, Mary Griffin, age seventy, who may be a former slave of Fitzhugh.[7] Naturally, more research would be needed to confirm or negate this theory.

It is also extremely important for descendants of slaves to learn the state laws of inheritance during a given time period and whether the slaves were considered real or personal property. For example, Maryland and South Carolina slaves were considered personal property; in Virginia in 1705, the law was changed to make slaves real property for purposes of inheritance.[8] When a woman married, all of her property, real and personal, became her husband's. But what happened to the slaves when he died? If there was a surviving will, it will likely tell you. But what if there was no will? Did the slaves become her property, or were they distributed to other heirs? Did she gain absolute title, meaning she could bequeath them to whomever she wanted at her death? Or did she receive only a life interest, which terminated upon her death? And what happened if the widow remarried and then she died? Did the slaves go to the second husband and his heirs, or to her heirs from her first marriage? As you can see, this can be a complex problem, but in cases where you cannot find a will that tells you who inherited your ancestors, you must study the laws of inheritance to determine which direction your research should take.

Along with the deeds and wills of whites who owned slaves, newspapers are another valuable source for tracing African American families. Runaway slaves were often advertised, giving physical descriptions. Some of the advertisements have been published in Lathan A. Windley's *Runaway Slave Advertisements: A Documentary History From the 1730s to 1790.*

Plantation records, if still in existence, may be another helpful source. Some slave owners recorded not only the sales and ownership of their slaves, but births, marriages and deaths. These records may be found among manuscript collections in state libraries and archives (check the *National Union Catalog of Manuscript Collections* mentioned in chapter one). Some have been microfilmed and made available at the Family History Library in Salt Lake City, Utah, or through microfilm rental from one of its family history centers worldwide. Others may be published, such as *South Central Kentucky Vital Statistics: Births and Deaths for Slaves and Black Families*, by Michelle Bartley Gorin.

After slaves were emancipated, you may find that blacks were segregated even in historical documents, such as marriage records. Even city directories may have a separate section in the back of the book that lists people of color. For the time period after the war, also look for slave narratives that were recorded and published by the Works Progress Administration of the 1930s.

Another record to consider is pension records from the Civil War; more than 100,000 African American men served. Because slave marriages were not considered legal, Congress made an adjustment in the requirement for presenting a legal document when a black veteran or his widow applied for a pension (see Appendix A on women's legal status).[9] As seen in the section in chapter two on pension applications, these records contain a wealth of information on the veteran, his widow and their families.

The Freedmen's Bureau, established in 1865, contains bureau reports and labor disputes that could aid in researching black women. Women hired as domestics could bring a dispute to the Freedmen's Bureau if their employers made them do work not stipulated in their contracts or agreements.[10]

Since they were excluded from white women's groups, black women formed their own clubs and organizations after the war. The National Association of Colored Women (NACW) was founded in 1896 and had more than three dozen chapters in twelve states and Washington, DC. By the early 1900s, black women had formed their own suffrage organizations in cities such as Tuskegee, St. Louis, Los Angeles, Memphis, Boston, Charleston and New Orleans. There were also state-level associations.[11]

For genealogical research on African Americans in general, see David T. Thackery's "Tracking African American Family History" in Loretto Dennis Szucs and Sandra Hargreaves Luebking's *The Source: A Guidebook of American Genealogy* and David Streets's *Slave Genealogy: A Research Guide With Case Studies*, as well as others listed in the Bibliography.

Native American Women

Along with the traditional censuses that the federal government took every ten years, there are special "Indian" enumerations. These schedules give the name of the tribe; the federal reservation; the agency; the nearest post office; the number in the household; the type of dwelling; and for each member of the household, the person's given name and an English translation, the relationship to the head of the household, marital status, tribal status, occupation, health, education and land ownership.

Technically, the 1870 federal population census was the first to designate Native Americans in the "color" column with an "I." Prior to that census year, enumerators for 1850 and 1860 were instructed to record only White ("W"), Black ("B") or Mulatto ("M"), although you may find exceptions in these censuses where an "I" is recorded.

Native Americans were enumerated on the 1880 federal census just like the general population, but for the 1900 and 1910 censuses, there are special schedules found among the regular population schedules that enumerate them separately. These are called "Inquiries Relating to Indians." In 1920, Native Americans were enumerated on the general population schedules and in a "Supplemental Schedule for Indian Population." These schedules are usually at the end of the censuses of the general population for each enumeration district.

From 1885 to 1940 censuses were taken of Native Americans by agents on each federal reservation. These were taken randomly, not annually. They are part of National Archives Record Group 75, Microcopy M595, 692 rolls. The *Indian Census Card Index* for 1898 to 1906 was compiled by the Dawes Commission to verify rights to tribal status for the Five Civilized Tribes (Cherokee, Chickasaw, Choctaw, Creek and Seminole). This index is available at the Family History Library in Salt Lake City, Utah, and at the National Archives regional branch in Fort Worth, Texas.

Of particular importance to tracing Native American women are the Indian School censuses taken by the Bureau of Indian Affairs between 1910 and 1939. These listed the names of children between the ages of six and eighteen years, their sex, tribe, degree of "Indian" blood, distance from home to school, parent or guardian, and attendance in school during the year. Often they will also include the maiden name of the mother. Many of the Indian schedules will give the given name and the English translation, such as *Na ka wo sa a*, also known as Agnes Fatwolf. These schedules are housed in the National Archives regional branch for the region where the school was located. Check Loretto Dennis Szucs and Sandra Hargreaves Luebking's *The Archives: A Guide to the National Archives Field Branches*.

Other sources on Native American genealogical research in general are Curt Witcher and George Nixon's "Tracking Native American Family History" in Szucs and Luebking's *The Source: A Guidebook of American Genealogy* and Edward Hill's *Guide to Records in the National Archives of the United States Relating to American Indians*.

The customs of each tribe are extremely important when researching female Native Americans. Some tribes place a greater importance on maternal ancestry and descent than paternal, and property is inherited through the mother's line. Learning the social history of the tribe, and about Native American women in general, is extremely valuable to your research. Two starting places would be Carolyn Niethammer's *Daughters of the Earth: The Lives and Legends of American Indian Women* and Gretchen M. Bataille and Kathleen Mullen Sands's *American Indian Women: Telling Their Lives*. Bataille and Sands's book has an excellent bibliography listing autobiographies, biographies, articles and books of and about Native American women.

You may also want to read "captivity narratives" written by white women who were kidnapped by various Indian tribes. Although they may be biased by white women's Christian values and morals, many of these firsthand accounts discuss their observations of Indian women and their daily lives. For references to some of these narratives, see June Namias's *White Captives: Gender and Ethnicity on the American Frontier* and Annette Kolodny's *The Land Before Her: Fantasy and Experience of the American Frontiers, 1630–1860*.

Jewish American Women

Along with the records from Chicago's Northwestern Hospital of Russian Jewish women and their pregnancies (see chapter two), another interesting source for Jewish women is a newspaper column called "The Bintel Brief" which was published in New York City's *Jewish Daily Forward*. Men and women wrote letters to the editor, some containing very personal items:

> I am a twenty-eight year old woman, married for six years and my only trouble is that I have no children. . . . My husband eats my heart out with a few words, like rust eats iron. He keeps saying it's "nearer than farther" to the ten-year limit when, according to Jewish law, I will have to give him a divorce if I don't have a baby by that time. . . . A short time ago I was quite sick and he spent a lot of money to cure me. When I got well my husband said to me, "You'll have to earn your own living, so I want you to be healthy."

> Dear Editor, I am all alone here, and I ask you to advise me what to do. Can my husband get a divorce after ten years through the court, too? I know he can get it through a rabbi. . . . How shall I act?[12]

The editor replied that the woman's husband could not obtain a legal divorce and that U.S. courts did not recognize rabbinical law. Other Jewish women probably experienced similar heartaches.

For women who read only Yiddish, this newspaper offered advice on assimilating into American culture. Isaac Metzker edited a book about these letters titled *A Bintel Brief: Sixty Years of Letters From the Lower East Side to the Jewish Daily Forward*. There was also a column in the *Forward* called "The Gallery of Missing Husbands," since desertion was a common problem among immigrant Jewish couples. Sometimes photographs of absent husbands were included. Even though you may not find your woman ancestor writing to "The Bintel Brief," it will give you a wonderful glimpse of that time period and how your women ancestors thought and felt.

For Jewish genealogical research in general, see *Avotaynu: The International Review of Jewish Genealogy* (155 North Washington Avenue, Bergenfield, New Jersey 07621). This quarterly journal is devoted to Jewish and east European research. Also see Gary Mokotoff's *How to Document Victims and Locate Survivors of the Holocaust* and Mokotoff's "Tracking Jewish-American Family History" in Szucs and Luebking's *The Source: A Guidebook of American Genealogy*.

Look also for social histories of Jewish women, such as Jacob Rader Marcus's *The American Jewish Woman, 1654–1980* and Sydney Stahl Weinberg's *The World of Our Mothers: The Lives of Jewish Immigrant Women*, which may lead you to more sources and which will help when you are ready to write a biography.

No matter what ethnic background your female heritage comprises, sources are available for research. By reading the social histories of an ethnic group, you can learn about records for which you may not have been previously aware. But regardless of heritage, one of the most common problems facing researchers is determining their female ancestors' maiden names and parents. This is the topic of the next chapter.

CHAPTER FOUR

Methods for Determining Maiden Names and Parents

Elizabeth was a member of the large and illustrious Blank family.

John I. Coddington

————— ◆◆ —————

Probably the most common problem in researching women is that of identity. What was her maiden name? Who were her parents? In some circumstances, you may know a woman's maiden name but not the names of her parents. Or you may have only her first name, so on your charts she is known as "Mary————." Or you may not know her name at all: "Jacob Hess married————." You may begin to feel as John Coddington, one of the leaders in the field of genealogy, felt when he referred in a lecture to Elizabeth————, "a member of the large and illustrious Blank family." While the maiden names and parents of some women on your pedigree may be easily found on a death certificate, in an obituary, in a family Bible, in a baptismal record or in a published genealogy, the further back in time you go, the harder it usually is to find the answers.

In some circumstances, a woman chose to keep her maiden name instead of using her husband's name. Lucy Stone (1819–93), a woman's rights advocate of the nineteenth century, was one of the first women to insist upon keeping her name when she married. Those who followed her lead were called "Lucy Stoners." In a short article in *The American Genealogist*, "Maiden Names Used After Marriage," the late George H.S. King,[1] a respected Virginia genealogist, noted that in some Virginia marriage and parish records, "ladies' names [were] entered in an almost unexplainable manner. I understand that in certain Quaker recordings the maiden names of brides have been used when they were widows." The editor of *The American Genealogist* added, "The practice here discussed is very common in Dutch records, maiden names and especially patronymics being used after many years of widowhood!" As mentioned in chapter two under Passenger Arrival Lists, Catholic French and Italian women in particular were known by their maiden names on all legal documents in their native lands. While this custom may not have been practiced once they came to America, all records generated in the Old Country—such as passenger lists and emigration papers—will record the woman by her maiden name.

Solving Identity Problems

Many genealogists have found ways of solving identity problems about women and have published their results. Reading published case studies on researching females found in the respected genealogical journals, such as the *National Genealogical Society Quarterly* (*NGSQ*), *The American Genealogist* (*TAG*), *The Genealogist* and *The New England Historical and Genealogical Register* (*The Register*), will give you ideas and involve you in the research process that helped solve some convoluted cases. Of these articles, many deal with colonial and early national women, especially those cases found in *TAG* and *The Register*. Some case studies are listed here in the Bibliography, but there are many more available. I encourage you to read and study many of these articles as you begin tracing women ancestors. Even though an article may not pertain specifically to your ancestry, the methods and sources the author used may help you solve a difficult research problem.

Several prominent genealogists have research theories on how to solve identity problems concerning female ancestors. Patricia Law Hatcher used a three-step process in her article "Mary Hale, Wife of Deacon Edward Putnam, Accuser in the Salem Witchcraft Trials":[2]

1. Identify all reasonable possibilities.
2. Eliminate all but one of the possibilities.
3. Identify and strengthen links to support the remaining possibility.

Elizabeth Shown Mills in a lecture titled "Finding Females: Wives, Daughters, Mothers, Sisters, and Paramours!" says you should reconstruct the lives of all the males associated with the woman: her husband, father, son and brother. By analyzing the data on these men and their relatives, classmates, business partners, military buddies, community associates and neighbors, you will also find information about the women.[3]

Sandra Hargreaves Luebking suggests in her lecture "Finding Females on the Frontier: Records and Strategies Using Nineteenth-Century Midwest Examples" that researchers first identify the specific problem (origin, identity, disappearance), then fix the woman in time and place with a known fact closest to the problem. For example, if a known fact is the birth of a child or a marriage, begin your search at that time and locality.[4]

All agree with historian Elizabeth Fox-Genovese that you must study women's relationships with men and with other women to "get at" the woman of interest. In other words, research everyone associated or connected with your woman ancestor. All also agree that you need to seek original records whenever possible rather than relying on published abstracts and transcriptions of records or published genealogies.

In many cases, you may never find that magic document that says, "I leave to my daughter, Ann," or, "Samuel and Martha (Richards) Montgomery are the parents of Penelope," which proves her parentage. Sometimes it is necessary to build a case based on the *evidence* you have gathered. In other words, make an inference about the unknown based on the known. Let's look at two cases to see how this works.

Case Studies

The Identity of Henry D. Bane's Wife, Nancy———

You may remember Nancy from chapter two under the discussion of insane asylums. I first found Nancy on the 1880 Schedule of Defective, Dependent, and Delinquent Classes for Gallia County, Ohio. My next step was to find her with her family to learn as much about her and her family as possible. On the 1880 population census for Gallia County the family is listed as follows:

> Bane, Henry D., white, male, age 61, married, farmer, born in Virginia, parents born in Virginia
>
> Bane, Nancy, white, female, age 62, wife, married, keeps house, mark under insane column, born in Ohio, parents born in Virginia
>
> Bane, William H., white, male, age 29 son, single, teacher, born in Ohio, father born in Virginia, mother born in Ohio[5]

Following Nancy in the censuses, I worked backward and forward in order to put together her family. Interestingly, in 1870, Nancy is also labeled as insane, but in 1860 and 1850, there were no remarks about Nancy's mental health.[6]

The Bane family is reconstructed here through the use of census records:

> Henry D. Bane was born September 1819 in Virginia. He married Nancy———, who was born September 1818 or 1819 in Ohio. They married about 1842.

Probable children (all born in Ohio):

    i. Lucetta, born about 1842

    ii. Samuel, born about 1845

    iii. John P., born about 1847

    iv. William H., born about 1850

    v. Mary A., born about 1853

    vi. Robert R., born about 1855

Since all of their children were born in Ohio, and they consistently lived in Gallia County, my next step was to see if a marriage record existed for Henry and Nancy in that area; it did. In the county marriage records, it was recorded that Henry D. Bane married Nancy Donnally on 26 September 1842.[7]

That was easy. Now we have what is likely her maiden name. (Remember, there is always the possibility that she could have been married before; her age when she married Henry calculates to about twenty-three.) As was common for marriage records for this time period, her parents' names were not included.

Assuming Donnally was Nancy's maiden name, it would make this a "quick case" if a man or woman named Donnally died in Gallia County and named a daughter Nancy Bane in a will. But of the Donnally wills, none named a daughter Nancy Bane. The will of Andrew Donnally did name a daughter Nancy, but referred to her as Donnally; "our" Nancy had been married thirteen years by the time this will was made in 1855, so it is unlikely that a father would still refer to his daughter by her maiden name. Another daughter and a son named in Andrew's will, Katherine and Peter

Donnally, also left wills in 1866 and 1860, respectively, naming their sister Nancy Donnally, giving further evidence this Nancy was unmarried.[8]

So this wasn't going to be so easy after all. Let's work on the approach that researching Nancy's husband may point us in the right direction. The chancery court records for Gallia County, 1835–52, have been abstracted and published. In the index, there was one case that involved Henry D. Bane and a John A. Donnally. It was a land foreclosure that also named Henry's wife, Nancy.[9]

Now to check the index for Donnallys. Of particular note was another court case of John Newton vs. John A. Donnally on 14 May 1840. In this case, as you may recall from the short discussion in chapter two, Orphan's and Guardianship Records, William Donnally was still living and owned land. He had the land conveyed to his children to defraud Newton. The children of William Donnally were named in the document: John A. and *Nancy*, who were of full age, and William Jr., Eleanor, Sarah, Mary Ann, Philip J., Martha, Reuben G. and Marinda, all minors.[10]

Two other significant cases were also noted. Again, one involved John A. Donnally, and a Sarah Donnally. This case stated that Sarah was the widow of William Donnally, who died 1 January 1847.[11] The other case was John Newton, administrator for William Grayum, vs. James Grayum, Reuben Grayum, John Grayum, Sarah and William Donnally, Martha and Randall Russell, Mary Ann and Noah Wood, and Rachel and John Swindler. This case of 1839 revolved around William Grayum dying intestate (without a will), and the need to sell his property to pay his debts. The people named were his brothers and sisters and his widow, Rachel, who married John Swindler.[12]

In the deeds, there was one land transaction between Henry D. Bane and the Donnallys—the one referred to in the foreclosure.[13] Deeds were also recorded that showed transactions between the Donnallys and James Newton and the Grahams [Grayum].[14] Aside from the deed of William Donnally conveying land to his children, which named a Nancy Donnally, there were no other solid familial connections.

Perhaps there was a death certificate for Nancy that would name her parents. According to a book of cemetery transcriptions for Gallia County, Nancy Bane, wife of Henry D., was born on 6 September 1818 and died 31 January 1903.[15] Ohio did not require state vital registration of deaths until 1908, but some earlier deaths were recorded in the county probate courts. Only Henry's death was on file. He died a widower at the age of eight-five on 23 February 1905.[16]

Recall the 1840 court case involving a Nancy Donnally who was of legal age. If Nancy (Donnally) Bane was the Nancy Donnally, daughter of William, then a birth date of September 1818 (from her tombstone) would have made her twenty-two years old in 1840, well above legal age. The 1900 census gave her birth month and year as September 1819, which would make her twenty-one in 1840. Of course, we have no way of knowing which is correct, if either one.

Let's take this one step further and see if William Donnally has a woman Nancy's age living in his household in the 1840 census.[17] Remember, this census named only the head of the household:

> males: 1 age under 5; 1 age 10–15; 1 age 15–20, 1 age 20–30, 1 age 40–50
> females: 2 age under 5; 1 age 5–10; 2 age 10–15; 1 age 15–20, 1 age 50–60

The only place where Nancy would fit is in the age category 15–20. From the above sources, however, she should be twenty-one or twenty-two. But there's something else we need to consider: the official starting date of the 1840 census was 1 June. The enumerator was supposed to record the composition of the household on that date, regardless of when he made his visit. If the birth month and year of September 1819 are correct, then Nancy would not turn twenty-one until September, making her twenty years old on 1 June 1840, when the census was taken.

In summary, we know:

- Nancy's presumed maiden name was Donnally from her marriage record to Henry D. Bane.
- Nancy named a son William.
- Henry D. and Nancy Bane were sued by a John A. Donnally.
- John A. Donnally had a sister named Nancy who was of full age in 1840, which coincided with Nancy (Donnally) Bane's age based on her tombstone inscription and the 1900 census.
- John A. and Nancy Donnally's father was William Donnally.
- William Donnally had living in his household in 1840 a woman of the right age to be Nancy.
- John A. Donnally was also involved in a suit with Sarah Donnally, who was the widow of William.
- Another court case cited Sarah and William Donnally, with Sarah being a sister of William Grayum, giving us her maiden name.

Thus, based on the evidence gathered, we can infer that Nancy was more than likely the daughter of William Donnally, possibly by his wife Sarah.

The Identity of Jesse Curry's Wife, Mary G.———

Jesse and Mary G. Curry were born in Green County, Kentucky. Census records from 1850 through 1870 show a prolific family. They had at least ten children, all also born in Green County:

Martha E.	born about 1840
Mary L.	born about 1842
William H.	born about 1844
Robert W.	born about 1846
James T.	born about 1847
John F.	born about 1852
Sallie	born about 1853
Sarah L.	born about 1856
Dorinda G.	born about 1859
Woodson [female]	born about 1860[18]

Once again, all that was needed to discover Mary's maiden name was a quick look at marriage records for Green County, Kentucky: Jesse Curry married Mary Strader. A bond was posted on 9 December 1839 by Richard Strader. The couple was married 10 November 1839 [*sic*] by the Reverend Stephen Gupton.[19] This record had an interesting bit of information. Notice that a Richard Strader posted the bond. Usually a father posted a bond on the bride's behalf. If he was deceased, the mother, an older brother or an uncle might post bond. Was Richard her father?

Published abstracts of wills for Green County were checked first; none was recorded for a Richard Strader.[20] In case the abstractor had missed Richard, I went to the original records and indexes. No, Richard hadn't left a will that was recorded.[21]

The next step was to look at the census records to see if this Richard was even the right age to be Mary's father. The 1850 Green County census (the first census to list everyone in the household by name) enumerated several Strader households. Of the heads of families, only Richard was old enough to be her father; he was sixty-one.[22] Of course, there is the possibility that Richard was an uncle, but what was particularly noteworthy were the names of Richard's wife and the children in his household: His wife was Martha, and the children were named Dorinda (age twenty-five), Martha (age twenty-three) and Thomas (age twenty-one). Mary and Jesse Curry named children Martha and Dorinda.

Though Jesse and Mary were married in 1839, there was no enumeration for them in the 1840 census in Green County, Kentucky, where Jesse might have been listed as a head of a household.

Let's take the census back one decade earlier when Mary would have been in Richard's household:[23]

Richard Strader
males: 1 aged under 5; 2 aged 5–10;
    1 aged 15–20; 1 aged 40–50
females: 2 under 5; 2 aged 5–10; 2
    aged 15–20; 1 aged 40–50

Calculating from the 1850 through 1870 censuses, Mary would have been born between 1817 and 1819, making her between the ages of eleven and thirteen in 1830. Without knowing the month she was born, she might fit in the five to ten-year-old category, being ten years old, but not yet turning eleven. Based on the 1850 census listing for Richard's household, his child Dorinda would have been five in 1830, Martha age three and Thomas, one. The other members of the household are unknown, but Richard and his wife were likely the ones age forty to fifty, which corresponded to their ages in the 1850 schedule.

In sum, we know:

- Jesse Curry's wife was Mary G. Strader.
- Richard Strader posted a bond for that marriage.
- Richard Strader was of the right age to be Mary's father.
- Mary named one child Martha, which was Richard's wife's name, and one

child Dorinda, which was the name of one of Richard's daughters.

- Richard had in his household in 1830 a daughter who may be the right age to be Mary.

Unless further research uncovers other possibilities, we can infer from this limited evidence that Mary G. (Strader) Curry was possibly the daughter of Richard Strader, probably by his wife Martha.

Other Genealogists' Methods for Identifying Women

Glade Ian Nelson, accredited genealogist and manager of the International Operations at the Family History Library in Salt Lake City, Utah, found the names of a woman's parents among her brother's Civil War records:

> Early in my genealogical research I attempted to find the parents of my third great-grandmother Angeline King, born 25 November 1813, in Kingtown (now Covert), Cayuga (now Seneca) County, New York. She married Ebenezer C. Richardson about 1833 in Greenwood, Steuben County, New York, but soon left with her husband and many of his extended family for Kirtland, Ohio. Many moves later found her in Plain City, Weber County, Utah, where she died 10 April 1880.
>
> Following extensive research, I determined that the preponderance of evidence indicated she and her identified fourteen brothers and sis-

ters were children of Ebenezer M. King and his wife Elizabeth or Betsy "surname unknown." For thirty years, "surname unknown" has graced my ancestral pedigree chart. I obtained a death certificate of Angeline's brother William, which verified he was a son of Ebenezer and Elizabeth "J." King.

> Recently I was made aware of a record newly acquired in the Family History Library in Salt Lake City. It is the New York "Town clerk's registers of men who served in the Civil War" (thirty-seven microfilm reels numbered 1992401–437). Shortly after the Civil War began, the town clerks in New York state were provided forms to complete on war registrants. The forms provided space for wonderful genealogical data—if only the town clerks would complete them, and—if only they would survive the more than a century since being distributed. Aware that Angeline's younger brothers were of the age to have served in the Civil War, I enthusiastically searched the records.
>
> The records from Greenwood revealed that Angeline's brother Silas L. served in the war. The information was incomplete, but it identified him as a son of Ebenezer King. Adjoining towns were next searched, and in West Union I hit the jackpot! The town clerk completed every requested data item including complete birth date, birth place and parents, as well as military service information

for Angeline's brother Edgar B. He was born 21 March 1826 in Trumansburg, Tompkins County, New York, whereas before I had an "about 1825" birth date based on census records. Only an imaginary line divides Trumansburg from Covert. Edgar was listed as the son of Ebenezer M. King and Elizabeth Jaycox!

No longer do I have a "surname unknown" for the mother of my third great-grandmother, Angeline King. Extensive direct research on Elizabeth or Betsy had been fruitless. Coming in the side door provided the needed information. Now I need to find the parents of Elizabeth Jaycox!

Anita Lustenberger, a Certified Genealogist in Irvington, New York, solved one woman's identity problem through the sale of slaves:

> Though it may be distasteful, the sale or distribution of slaves in order to pay debts and distribute the proceeds to the heirs provides relationships and maiden names. Elias DeJarnette died in 1824. In 1842, the slaves in the estate were appraised and distributed to Permelia Jones, Elizabeth Cally, Lucretia Littlepage, Madison DeJarnette, William Spencer, John Spencer, Edward Tarrant, Samuel H. VanZant, and John T. VanZant. The first three women were daughters of Elias DeJarnette. Further research showed the last five men were the sons-in-law and sons of

the late Sophia (DeJarnette) VanZant. Eventually, the first names of the three VanZant daughters were found. This document led to the maiden names of seven women, in two generations.

In another case, Lustenberger found a woman's maiden name using cemetery records:

> In the Samuel Reynolds plot, Allegheny Cemetery, Pittsburgh, Pennsylvania, there are headstones for Samuel and his wife, Hannah (1815–1895). According to the 1850 and later censuses, both were born in England. I visited the cemetery office to obtain a copy of the family plot. I was surprised to find it included the burials of two people who had no tombstones. Mary Ford and Benjamin Ford had died in 1868 and 1870, respectively, aged 84 and 92, and both had been interred in Allegheny Cemetery on 11 December 1891. They were found on the 1860 census, both born in England, enumerated a few pages away from the Samuel Reynolds household, and then in city directories on the same street. Other evidence confirmed the identity of Hannah (Ford) Reynolds. Now there is a new question: Who was Mary (———) Ford?

And in this case, Lustenberger was happy just to discover a woman's first name:

> A published abstract of wills for Richland District, South Carolina, had

provided the maiden name of Mary Caroline (Walker) Tarrant, and gave her siblings as Fanny, Elisabeth, and James Alexander Walker. All were the children of Edward Walker, who wrote his will in 1800. Eventually the packet of loose papers for the estate was examined. Edward seems to have died about 1803. One paper discussed the support of Edward Walker's *two* sons: Frederick Walker had been born after the will was written. Another paper referred to the widow, proving that Mrs. Walker had survived her husband. And another referred to her as *Lucy* Walker, providing the first usage of her first name. Though I haven't found her maiden name yet, it is much easier to search for Lucy (————) Walker than ———— (————) Walker!

Marcia Wyett, a Certified Genealogical Record Specialist in Colorado Springs, Colorado, discovered a gold mine when searching for a female:

> The family tradition was that Sarah McMahill and George Holliday were married in Warren County, Illinois, in 1832. Sarah's father was John McMahill, and she was born in 1813 in Kentucky.
>
> There was no marriage record for Sarah and George in Warren County, Illinois, and there was no additional information about Sarah's parents. A county history for Warren County recorded a George W. McMahill born in

Kentucky in 1826. His father's name was John and [he was] also a native of Kentucky. George's grandfather was also named John. Here was the first concurring information with Sarah McMahill: both Sarah and George W. were born in Kentucky, both were contemporaries, both had fathers named John, and both lived in Warren County, Illinois.

A search of the 1850 census for Warren County revealed four McMahill families living near one another:

Family #593: John McMahill, age 32, born Kentucky

Family #594: Jefferson McMahill, age 25, born Kentucky; also in the household was Susan McMahill, widow, age 62, born in Virginia

Family #595: George W. McMahill, age 27, born Kentucky

Family #599: William McMahill, age 43, born Kentucky

Sarah named her only daughter Susan, which makes the widow Susan McMahill a likely candidate for Sarah's mother. In a twelve-volume set of tombstone transcriptions for Warren County, I found a McMahill Cemetery. Among the inscriptions was one for "Susan McMahill, wife of John, died October 1, 1867."

Another Warren County history named Jefferson McMahill as being born in Nicholas County, Kentucky.

Now I had a more specific location to check. The grantor and grantee indexes to deeds for Nicholas County from 1806–63 revealed several transactions by McMahills. In particular, one land sale was for Susan McMahill, and two entries were for a William. Susan's entry was a dower release, stating that she was the widow of John, and was dated April 28, 1832. So I now knew that John died before this date in Kentucky.

One of the deeds for William McMahill provided considerable information; in fact, three generations were listed. The entry is an indenture dated 12 June 1827 between Ambrose Barnett and William McMahill Jr., both of Nicholas County, Kentucky. The land record begins, "Ambrose Barnett for and in consideration of the natural love and affection which he the said Ambrose Barnett bears and hath for him the said William McMahill Jr. and for consideration of the sum of $1.00." Further in the record, it stated, "being part of the land on which John McMahill now lives. . . . " [This was the property for which Susan released her dower in 1832; so John's death can be narrowed to between 12 June 1827 and 28 April 1832.]

The record further stated that the land transaction is for a term of twenty years from the date of record, "at expiration of 20 year term premises are to be equally divided amongst all the brothers and sisters of said William McMahill Jr. to wit: Ambrose, Louisa, Robert, *Sarah*, James, John, Henry, Washington, and Jefferson McMahill all heirs and legal representatives of that John McMahill may have by his wife Susan late Susan Barnett."

I now had Sarah McMahill with parents John and Susan (Barnett) McMahill, names of her siblings, and a possible grandparent, Ambrose Barnett (Sarah also named a son Barnett). Further research may reveal that Susan (Barnett) McMahill was the daughter of Ambrose Barnett.

The following is how Ann Lainhart, a professional genealogist in Peabody, Massachusetts, found the maiden name of a colonial woman:

> In the *Alden Memorial*, published in 1901, the wife of a John Alden of Boston is given as "Elizabeth, daughter of William Phelps, senior." Two years ago I tried to confirm this identification without success, but it was not until reading through baptisms of the Old South Church that I came across the clue that led to the probable identification of John's wife's maiden name.
>
> There is no marriage record for John Alden and his wife Elizabeth. She was the mother of all John's children from 1687 through 1710, and she died on 26 November 1719 at the age of 50, thus making her born about

1669. Among their children there is one unusual naming pattern: twins named Gillam and Ann were born in Boston on 7 July 1699 and baptized in Old South Church on 9 July 1699. While reading through the baptisms at Old South, I found the family of Benjamin and Hannah Gillam, who were having children baptized from 1671 to 1682.

I first thought that John's wife might therefore be Elizabeth Gillam but could find no birth record for one born about 1669. I did find Elizabeth Gillam, daughter of Benjamin and Ann (———) Gillam, who married Thomas Gwinn about 1660 and had Elizabeth, born 16 October 1668. Here was an Elizabeth born about the same time as John Alden's wife and connected to the Gillam family.

John Alden's wife was born at the same time as this Elizabeth Gwinn, daughter of Thomas and Elizabeth (Gillam) Gwinn. John Alden and his wife Elizabeth were members of the same church as Benjamin and Hannah (———) Gillam and Thomas and Sarah (Dixey) Gwinn.

The Alden and Gillam families certainly knew each other since John's mother, Elizabeth (Phillips) Alden, and Elizabeth Gwinn's aunt, Phebe (Phillips) Gillam, were sisters. Benjamin Gillam was a wealthy shipwright while both John and his father were shipmasters, so they may have had business ties.

Besides naming children Gillam and Ann, three of John and Elizabeth's other children's names are significant and do not appear in the families of John's father or grandfather: Hannah, who would have been named for Elizabeth's aunt, Hannah (Gillam) Sharp, who raised her; Katherine, who would have been named for Elizabeth's cousin, Katherine Sharp, daughter of Richard and Hannah (Gillam) Sharp; and Thomas, who would have been named for Elizabeth's father and brother, Thomas Gwinn.

Finally, Roger D. Joslyn, Certified Genealogist and Fellow of the American Society of Genealogists, in New Windsor, New York, shows how a twice-married woman's identity was solved through deeds and circumstantial evidence [for more details on this case, see Joslyn's article "Abigail (Wells) (Wetmore) Seward of Durham, Connecticut: Wife of Jabez Wetmore and Ephraim Seward," *The American Genealogist* 72 (1997): 81–88]:

Abigail was the problem. Her marriage, as Abigail Wetmore, to Ephraim Seward is found in Durham, Connecticut, 1743, but no birth of an Abigail Wetmore in that area roughly sixteen to thirty years earlier is evident. One possible explanation was she was married before, and indeed Jabez and Abigail Wetmore were having children in Durham up to 1740, but no marriage of this couple was found.

Durham deeds solved the problem of Abigail's identity: In 1775, five days before his death, Jonathan Wells of Durham conveyed land there to his daughter Abigail, wife of Ephraim Seward. When Ephraim Seward and his wife Abigail sold the same property four years later, she was again described as Jonathan Wells's daughter.

That Abigail was first married to Jabez Wetmore is proved circumstantially—through chronology, naming patterns, and the associations between the families of her children by both husbands.

Every genealogist tackles women's identity problems differently, depending on the time period, locality and ethnic group. This is why it is so important to read case studies; one of these strategies may work for you. All of the above cases prove that you just never know what record will reveal the information you need to identify a woman. Leave no stone unturned! But once you have exhausted the genealogical sources, don't stop there. Thus far, you have completed only the first step in the recipe for researching and writing about your female ancestors. Now it's time for step two, where you combine your genealogical research with information you'll find in women's social histories.

CHAPTER FIVE

Writing About Women Ancestors

We see our ancestors as we wish they were—peaceful and loving—rather than as they really were—human and often contentious.

Glenda Riley in
Divorce: An American Tradition

As mentioned in the Introduction, genealogical records are only some of the ingredients in the search for your female ancestor's life story. These usually give you the names, dates and places. If you find letters, diaries or some other detailed sources, you may be able to put together a short, interesting biography. Sometimes, however, genealogical records leave gaps in a woman's life story; the information does not tell you what her life was like. To complete the picture, let's look at how to reconstruct your women ancestors' lives by adding social history research and ultimately writing a biographical narrative.

Women's Social History

Social histories tell about everyday people and their daily lives, as opposed to military histories that discuss wars, political histories that detail politics or even traditional histories that focus on famous, national events and people. Women's social histories, therefore, detail the typical experience and daily activities of ordinary women.

Social historians use the same sources as genealogists: wills and inventories, court records, land and tax records, letters and diaries, and oral history interviews. The difference is that social historians focus on the community as a whole, while we genealogists focus on individuals or specific families. From the historians' research of the whole community, we can learn about the common or typical daily life experience. This is the kind of information we need to supplement the data we learn about our female ancestors through genealogical research. Social histories can be found in public and, in particular, university libraries, and in new and used bookstores.

Begin by reading general women's history books, which discuss all classes and races of women, such as Sara M. Evans's *Born for Liberty: A History of Women in America*, Carol Hymowitz and Michaele Weissman's *A History of Women in America* or Carl N. Degler's *At Odds: Women and the Family in America From the Revolution to the Present.*

Then move on to more specific social histories about women in a given time or place, such as Herbert Gutman's *The Black Family in Slavery and Freedom, 1750–1925*, Glenda Riley's *Women and Indians on the Frontier, 1825–1915* or Carol Bleser's *In Joy and in Sorrow: Women, Family, and Marriage in the Victorian South, 1830–1900.*

Believe it or not, the extensive bibliography in this book only scratches the surface on the types of books you can find. But these will give you a good starting place; in these books, look at the notes and bibliographies to find more. There are social histories written about all classes and ethnic backgrounds of women and for all time periods.

Look for women's social histories in your library's computer catalog. Type in key words such as "Women—United States History" or "Women—United States History—Education" or "Afro-American Women—History" or "Indians of North America—Women." In new and used bookstores, there is usually a section devoted to women's studies, but also look in the American history section.

There are also journals and articles published about women's history. One periodical in particular is *Journal of Women's History* (Indiana University Press, 601 North Morton Street, Bloomington, Indiana 47404). Bibliographies, such as Cynthia Harrison's *Women in American History: A Bibliography,* which surveys more than seven thousand articles on American and Canadian women's history, will help you find specific materials. Another source is Gayle Fischer's *Journal of Women's History: Guide to Periodical Literature*, a bibliogra-

phy of more than 750 journals from 1980 through 1990, listing more than 5,500 articles arranged by forty topics, such as African American Women, Education, Ethnicity, Friendship, Law/Crime and Marriage/Divorce, to name a few. Also check general history journals and magazines that would publish articles on women's studies. In 1987, Congress declared March Women's History Month, so you are likely to find articles on women's topics or a whole issue devoted to women's studies during this month. In addition, you may also want to pursue unpublished dissertations about women's history topics. See Victor Gilbert and Darshan Tatla's *Women's Studies: A Bibliography of Dissertations, 1870–1982.*

Along with social histories of women, there are general social histories that will give you additional information, such as David Freeman Hawke's *Everyday Life in Early America* and Judson Hale's *The Best of The Old Farmer's Almanac: The First 200 Years. The Old Farmer's Almanac* gave farm girls and women advice on many subjects, just as the prescriptive literature written specially for women did (see the section on Female Roles, page 67). The 1881 *Almanac* advised women when they should wean their babies. The 1867 issue told farmers' daughters that they should be able to sew and knit, to wash dishes and keep house, to keep their rooms neat and tidy, to entertain visitors if mother is not at home and to nurse the sick.

Another type of book that may offer motivations to your woman ancestor's actions are books on superstitions, customs and folklore. Ever wonder why widows wear black? Originally, widows were to wear black for up to seven years. Black clothes made women less visible to spirits. If she wore black, her dead husband would have trouble seeing her and coming back to pester her. Supplementing your narrative with customs, superstitions and folklore can make for a most interesting and colorful family history. Most ethnic groups have their own folk beliefs, and you could just as easily research those, too.

Social History Topics

There are many topics to explore that may be pertinent to your female ancestors. Some social histories may also lead you to records you did not know existed. After the topics below, I've listed some works you can consult if you would like more information; however, rarely are these the only books or articles on a particular subject. All are listed in the Bibliography along with references to other works.

Just as we analyzed the genealogical records in chapter two, as you read the overview of the topics, consider how each could have played a role in your female ancestors' lives. In other words, how would a particular topic affect your ancestor? Though you may not have letters, diaries, oral histories or genealogical documents to tell you whether or not one of your foremothers experienced something, do not automatically dismiss the topic. Given the commonality of a particular situation, you may be able to speculate on that aspect of an ancestor's life. For example, just as your descendants are

not likely to find a document telling them whether or not you used some form of contraceptive, we know that it is extremely common for childbearing-aged women today to use some method of limiting the number of children they have. Thus, we can speculate that any given woman living today who has only a few children *likely* used or continues to use a form of birth control. Likewise, it is doubtful you will find evidence of your female ancestor being addicted to patent medicines containing alcohol, opium or morphine. Yet historians have concluded that this was extremely common among women, especially upper-class Southern women. If your ancestor was an upper-class Southern woman, you can speculate that she *probably* used patent medicines on a regular basis. The wording you choose—*probably, likely, possibly, no doubt*—plus stating that this was a common experience based on scholarly historical research, lets your readers and descendants know that you are speculating. (See how the topic of drug use is handled in the biography of Mary Fitzhugh in the next chapter.)

Sexuality

Our foremothers went through the same stages of life as women today: menstruation, childbirth, menopause. How these three stages and others were viewed and accepted depended on the time period and ethnic or socioeconomic background of a woman. How women felt about their sexuality is attributable to society as well as cultural differences and historical era. Colonial Quaker women, because they were allowed more freedom to voice their opinions, no doubt had a better self-esteem than those in cultures and religions where women who spoke out were considered insane. This would be an interesting area to research for all of your female ancestors. In a family history, you could show how attitudes changed over the centuries and through the generations.

Another part of a woman's sexuality included how she viewed sex and reproduction. During the nineteenth century, most American women considered sex simply part of their wifely duties. Jewish American women, however, were raised to believe that the sex act should be enjoyable to both the husband and wife. In addition, in some groups and time periods, premarital sex was not necessarily taboo. One reason for the union of a couple was the production of heirs. This burden rested on whether the woman was able to conceive. If she wasn't, she might not make a good marriage partner, so weddings took place after the conception of a child.

Family planning also affected women from early history. In most marriages, recurrent childbirths were wanted and sought, no matter what toll it took on women's lives: often early death. Many women feared death from childbirth so much that they would do almost anything—from swallowing poisonous concoctions to inserting sharp objects such as buttonhooks or knitting needles into their wombs—to avoid carrying a child to term. Economics also played an important role in the limitation of family size. An agrarian household needed a large number of children to help on the farm; a low-income urban family confined to a two-room tenement apartment did not need extra mouths to feed. Birth control methods and abortions are as much a part of women's history as childbirth is. Abortions and birth control could also explain large intervals between the births of children.

Many women died from abortions, either from rupturing their uteruses and bleeding to death or from causing infection by using unsterile instruments. If a woman died from complications as a result of an abortion, the cause on a death certificate might be disguised. Uterine hemorrhaging, uterine cancer, septicemia, tetanus or any number of related or unrelated causes might appear because Victorian discretion often dictated a "respectable" diagnosis. (See Medical Records in chapter two.)

For more information on the topic of sexuality, see works such as John D'Emilio and Estelle B. Freedman's *Intimate Matters: A History of Sexuality in America*, James C. Mohr's *Abortion in America: The Origins and Evolution of National Policy, 1800–1900*, Linda Gordon's *Woman's Body, Woman's Right: A Social History of Birth Control in America* and my own article "Immigrant Women and Family Planning: Historical Perspectives for Genealogical Research" in the June 1996 *National Genealogical Society Quarterly*.

Childbearing and Child Raising

For the majority of our female ancestors, life revolved around home and family. Girls were raised to be wives and mothers. When they married, most couples had many children, which was necessary to foster a primarily agrarian society. Though it was not uncommon for women to fear childbirth, they still had frequent pregnancies when no other alternative was available to them. During the time of westward migration, one out of five women was in some stage of pregnancy when she made the journey with her husband. While women were generally attended by midwives and female relatives during childbirth, for some rural women isolated on the frontier, giving birth could be a lonely and frightening experience. By the time her husband unhitched the horse from the plow and went to a neighbor's for help, she could have already delivered her baby.

Babies and small children were often victims of contagious diseases and accidents. Though this was a common occurrence in families, the loss of a child was nonetheless heartbreaking for the mother and the rest of the family. In many cultures the use of necronyms—naming a newborn after a deceased child—was not only a means of preserving the naming pattern, but it also paid tribute to the child who had died. You may even find postmortem photographs of babies among your family possessions.

The woman was responsible for caring for and raising the children, as well as doing household chores. Once her daughters were old enough, she relied on them to help her with the younger children. Until the nineteenth century when birth control methods became more widely available and reliable, a woman spent the majority of her life giving birth and raising children. For all of your female ancestors, this is an important aspect when writing her biography. There are many social histories of childbearing and child raising. See works such as Judith Walzer Leavitt's *Brought to Bed: Childbearing in America, 1750–1950*, Catherine M. Scholten's *Childbearing in American Society, 1650–1850* and Sylvia D. Hoffert's *Private Matters: American Attitudes Toward Childbearing and Infant Nurture in the Urban North, 1800–1860*.

Bastardy and Infanticide

For the single, pregnant woman who did not see abortion as an option, there were two other alternatives: Name the father in court so that he could support the child, or resort to infanticide. Bastardy cases were common and are found among court proceedings (see chapter two, Court Records). Illegitimate children were a financial burden on the community, so officials often coerced a mother to name the father.

Infanticide, murdering one's baby, was a crime from before the founding of our country. Even if the child had been born dead, but the mother concealed her bastard infant's death, she was considered guilty of infanticide, unless she could prove otherwise. Women found guilty of this capital crime were put to death. In the South, some black slave women killed their babies to free them from future bondage and as a way of depriving their masters of more slaves.

The first known case of infanticide in this country was in Massachusetts and occurred in 1638. Dorothy Talbye was hung for murdering her three-year-old daughter, Difficult, by breaking the child's neck.[1] One young woman who lived with her parents in the 1690s, Elizabeth Emerson of Suffolk County, Massachusetts, buried her illegitimate children in the family's garden.[2] After the 1730s, convictions for infanticide declined. Where there was evidence, judges and juries were becoming more willing to accept stillbirth and accidental death, even if the death had been concealed.

So along with reading social histories, such as Ann Jones's *Women Who Kill* and Peter Hoffer and N.E.H. Hull's *Murdering Mothers: Infanticide in England and New England, 1558–1803*, which also cite names of women and cases, check newspapers and court records into the early nineteenth century.

Female Roles

How women were expected to behave plays a part in your family history as well. Girls were raised to become wives and mothers, the caretakers of their families' needs. Women's magazines, the Sunday newspaper's woman's section, advice books and novels published during your ancestor's lifetime will give you insights as to how she may have acted, what she may have worn and what was expected of her. As early as 1828, women's magazines began appearing on the market. *Godey's Lady's Book*, a journal begun in 1837, had a national circulation of 150,000 by 1860. This monthly magazine offered information on fashion, home-making, health matters, as well as published fiction, poetry and recipes. *Mme. Demorest's*

Mirror of Fashions, first published in 1860, reproduced tissue-paper dress patterns in each issue. For more progressive women of the late 1860s, a sixteen-page weekly newsletter, *Revolution*, covered all aspects of women's lives: food, fashion, health, marriage, work, unions, women in professions and trades, and notable women.

In addition to magazines, there was prescriptive domestic literature for every period of women's history in the form of books and novels (see the Source Checklist in Appendix C). One example was Lydia Child's 1829 guide, *The Frugal Housewife*, later called *The American Frugal Housewife*. Included were recipes for common dishes such as puddings, custards, pies, cakes and breads. Child also discussed home health remedies—"If you happen to cut yourself slightly while cooking, bind on some fine salt"—making soap, and using old scraps of items economically—"After old coats, pantaloons, &c. [etc.] have been cut up for boys and are no longer capable of being converted into garments, cut them into strips, and employ the leisure moments of children, or domestics, in sewing and braiding them for door-mats."

Women's roles often went beyond that of wife and mother. The woman was also expected to be a nurse for all types of illnesses and injuries. She cared for elderly parents and other disabled family members living in her household. If one of her children were deaf or blind, retarded, or afflicted with some other physical or mental handicap, she also provided the care and special attention required for that circumstance. If you find these situations in your ancestry—from your research in records, through oral history or mentioned in letters and diaries—also explore social histories that would discuss a woman's life regarding these areas.

Along with contemporary magazines and prescriptive literature, also see Nancy K. Humphreys's *American Women's Magazines: An Annotated Historical Guide* and Barbara Ehrenreich's and Deirdre English's *For Her Own Good: 150 Years of the Experts' Advice to Women.*

Women's Work

While the majority of women were housewives well into the twentieth century, in the nineteenth century women began working outside the home as schoolteachers, domestics, factory workers, seamstresses and nurses. The more women entered the new workplaces, especially after the Civil War and then during and after the two world wars, the more they dealt with unpleasant working conditions, which resulted in the formation of women's labor organizations. Women's historians have documented the lives of working women very well.

It was not uncommon for educated women to teach a year or two of school before they married. As early as the 1830s, women started entering the teaching profession; toward the end of the nineteenth century, this was *the* profession for middle-class women. The frontier one-room schoolhouses of the 1880s to 1950s employed more women than men, and the vast majority of all female schoolteachers—rural and urban—were young and single. The turnover rate was high, however, because when they married, the schoolteachers were expected to resign their position. Few women teachers had a complete college education; it was more common to have a normal-school education or just six to eight years of any formal schooling (see chapter two, School Records). Rural schoolteachers usually boarded with a family for the school term, and as late as 1915, they were expected to follow strict rules if they wished to remain employed:

1. Do not get married.
2. Do not leave town at any time without permission of the school board.
3. Do not keep company with men.
4. Be home between the hours of 8 P.M. and 6 A.M.
5. Do not loiter downtown in ice cream stores.
6. Do not smoke.
7. Do not get into a carriage with any man except your father or brother.
8. Do not dress in bright colors.
9. Do not dye your hair.
10. Do not wear any dress more than two inches above the ankle.[3]

Just as ethnic background influenced attitudes toward sexuality, it also was a factor when women began working inside and outside of the home. Italian married women, for example, preferred to work inside the home, doing piecework for factories that manufactured artificial flowers and trimmed hats. German and Bohemian women worked in their homes rolling cigars. Married Jewish women did needle-work in their homes. Irish and Scandinavian single women took jobs as domestics, while single Jewish and Italian women worked in factories. After the Civil War, because black males suffered from employment discrimination, their wives found it easier to find work as domestics. But unlike single Irish and Scandinavian women who lived in their employers' homes, married black women refused to do so; they had families at home to care for, and living where they worked reminded them of slavery.[4] Many black women in Illinois and Indiana were employed by the Pullman Company at the turn of the twentieth century.[5]

When women joined the workforce, sexual harassment became an increasing problem, especially in factories. Both immigrant women at the turn of the twentieth century and the large numbers of New England women who worked the mills of Massachusetts, New Hampshire, Vermont and Maine in the 1820s and 1830s experienced male bosses who demanded sexual favors.

For more details on working women, see works such as Susan Strasser's *Never Done: A History of American Housework*, Julia Weber Gordon's *My County School Diary*, David M. Katzman's *Seven Days a Week: Women and Domestic Service in Industrializing America* and Lynn Weiner's *From Working Girl to Working Mother: The Female Labor Force in the United States, 1820–1980*.

Drug Addictions

The majority of nineteenth-century morphine and opium addicts were native-born white women, with a heavy concentration among Southern middle and upper classes, which persisted into the early twentieth century. The typical morphine addict of the 1920s was a Southern white female, middle-aged or older, widowed, home-bound and a property owner. It was not uncommon for women to become addicted by their physicians who prescribed the medicine. According to David T. Courtwright's *Dark Paradise: Opiate Addiction in America Before 1940*:

> The most common occupation among female addicts was that of housewife. The majority of nineteenth-century female addicts were married and therefore stayed at home. Unmarried female addicts were observed among domestics, teachers, actresses, and especially prostitutes. Another type, mentioned as early as 1832, was the harried society lady, who downed opium or morphine to steady her nerve and enhance her wit. Women associated with the medical profession—nurses and doctors' wives—also had an unusually high rate of addiction.[6]

Southern plantation women as early as the 1850s commonly used opium as a base for many of their home remedies. Mary Chesnut, a typical upper-class Southern woman during the time of the Civil War, kept a diary in which she records her regular use of opium and morphine.[7] Historians consider Mary's diary to be one of the best sources for women's views and lives during this time.

Laudanum was another addictive drug that was in wide use in the nineteenth century and freely prescribed by doctors for "female complaints." It was used among middle- and upper-class women to relieve depression and insomnia. (Strange how history repeats itself: In the 1950s and 1960s physicians freely prescribed Valium to relieve women's depression; today it's Prozac for depression and premenstrual syndrome. Doctors still haven't figured out how to handle those "female complaints"!)

Since women were in charge of the family's medicine and home remedies, addictive drugs were a constant temptation. Patent medicines contained opium, morphine and/or alcohol. Lydia E. Pinkham's Vegetable Compound, for example, contained from 19 to 35 percent alcohol and could be purchased at local pharmacies and through mail-order advertisements in newspapers and magazines. Addictive patent medicines and syrups were also administered to babies; some were advertised specifically as infant pacifiers, such as Winslow's Baby Syrup and Kopp's Baby Friend, both of which contained morphine. Even heroin found its way into cough medicine manufactured by the Bayer company in 1898. Women of the nineteenth century who were treated in insane asylums (see chapter two) often left as drug addicts. Surviving letters and diaries may give clues to use of addictive drugs and patent medicines.

Besides Courtwright's book mentioned earlier, also see Stephen R. Kandall's *Substance and Shadow: Women and Addiction in the United States* and Sarah Stage's *Female Complaints: Lydia Pinkham and the Business of Women's Medicine.*

Religion and Spiritualism

Religion and spirituality played an important role in the lives of practically all women. Native American women, for example, had spiritual rituals unique to each tribe: Sioux women performed dances to entice buffalo, young women of the Menominee and Potowatomi tribes engaged in ritual fasts lasting more than a week to find their guardian spirits, and women of the Hidatsa tribe had ceremonies for good crops each year.

The Great Awakening of the 1730s and 1740s and the Second Great Awakening between 1798 and 1826 encouraged women's participation by forming prayer groups and revivals. In their religion and churches, women of many denominations were allowed to teach Sunday school, hold prayer meetings and, in a few cases, preach. Women formed missionary societies starting in 1868 with the founding of the Congregationalist's Woman's Board of Missions. During the nineteenth century, religious movements and spiritual revivals enticed thousands of women. Many women led such groups and founded new religions, such as Mary Baker Eddy, the founder of Christian Science, and Ann Lee of the Shakers. More women than men joined Shaker communities, which advocated celibacy. There were more than five thousand members by the 1830s.

The Quaker religion allowed women more freedom than most denominations. Quakers encouraged women to be leaders and ministers who would oversee other women's spiritual life. See the section on Quaker journals in chapter one, as well as Ellen Thomas and David Allen Berry's *Our Quaker Ancestors: Finding Them in Quaker Records*. Also see Church Records in chapter two.

See works such as Rosemary Ruether and Rosemary Keller's comprehensive three-volume work, *Women and Religion in America*, and Cynthia Grant Tucker's *Prophetic Sisterhood: Liberal Women Ministers of the Frontier, 1880–1930*.

Women's Rights and Moral Reform Movements

Mary Wollstonecraft's *A Vindication of the Rights of Women* published in 1792 sparked a long battle for women's rights. In the 1800s, her book was considered the "feminist bible" and was read by many women. Throughout our country's history, from slavery to education, women have been active leaders in the areas of reform and women's rights. In the 1830s, hundreds of women organized abolition groups in the North. The first women's rights convention was held in 1848 in Seneca Falls, New York, and not long afterward, women's groups formed in many states. At issue were married women's rights, divorce laws and suffrage.

Even those who did not actively participate were affected by the issues of women's rights and reform movements, and many signed petitions and kept informed by reading newspapers and magazines. (See chapter one, Legislative Petitions.) Middle- and upper-class Northern women, in particular, organized moral reform societies to abolish such evils as slavery and alcohol. In fact, Northern women were among the originators of the antislavery movements. In the South, though many women opposed slavery, it was difficult for them to form these types of movements. Later in the nineteenth century, however, Southern women began taking active roles in women's rights and reform movements.

The Women's Christian Temperance Union (WCTU) began in 1874, but there were women in Hillsboro, Ohio, and Adrian, Michigan, the year before who had begun the crusade for temperance. The women who participated in temperance movements sought to protect their homes and families from violence, indebtedness, desertion and the immorality caused by men's abuse of alcohol. Ironically, some of these women were addicted themselves to opiate- and alcohol-based patent medicines. Women from many walks of life were members of the WCTU: urban and rural, western and eastern, northern and southern, and lower, middle and upper classes. Not all women advocated temperance, however. For example, Catholics used wine in their sacraments, and the wives of enlisted men and officers stationed at isolated military forts in the West saw the need for alcohol consumption as part of the men's way of socializing and dealing with the isolation.

As the nineteenth century progressed,

millions of women participated in reform work that targeted education, prisons and health care, as well as formed and joined church activities, women's clubs and civic groups. In 1890, the General Federation of Women's Clubs was an umbrella group that "brought together 200 clubs representing 20,000 women. By 1900, it had 150,000 members and two decades later claimed to represent a million."[8]

For more on women's clubs and organizations, see Karen J. Blair's *The History of American Women's Voluntary Organizations, 1810–1960: A Guide to Sources*, Jane C. Croly's *The History of the Woman's Club Movement in America* and Ruth Bordin's *Woman and Temperance: The Quest for Power and Liberty, 1873–1900*.

The above topics are just a few areas of women's social history that you can explore to research the impact on your female ancestors. Other areas that are well covered in women's social histories are:

- nurses
- farm and rural women
- history of women's health and medical care
- history of prostitution
- various ethnic groups and races
- regional women
- women in the military (in wars and on the homefront)
- women in particular time periods

(The Roaring Twenties, the 1930s, the 1950s, the Progressive Era, etc.)
- women in the arts

Blending Social and Family History: Some Examples

Once you have researched your women ancestors and the social history surrounding their day and time, you can blend the two together to write biographies about your foremothers. Following are a few examples of combining social and family history that deal with women of different time periods and localities.

Cicely (Penny) Chapin: A Colonial New England Woman

This is what you might typically find in a published genealogy, except the husband is usually listed first instead of the wife:[9]

Cicely Penny was the daughter of Henry Penny of Paignton, England. She was baptized on 21 February 1601/2 in Paignton and died 8 February 1682/3 in Springfield, Massachusetts. Her will was dated 16 May 1676, and an inventory was taken 5 March 1682. Cicely was married on 9 February 1623/4 in Paignton to Deacon Samuel Chapin. Samuel was the son of John Chapin. He was baptized on 8 October 1598 in Paignton and died on 11 November 1675 in Springfield, Massachusetts. They came to Roxbury,

Massachusetts, about 1638, and settled in Springfield about 1642.

Children:

   i. David, baptized 4 January 1624/5, Paignton, England

   ii. Catherine, baptized 1626, Berry Pomeroy, England

   iii. Sara, baptized October 1628, Berry Pomeroy

   iv. son (probably born Samuel and a twin), baptized January 1630/1, Berry Pomeroy

   v. Henry (probably born twin), baptized January 1630/1, Berry Pomeroy

   vi. John, baptized 16 January 1632/3, Totnes, County Devon, England

   vii. Honor (daughter), baptized 8 May 1636, Berry Pomeroy

   viii. Josiah, baptized 29 October 1637, Berry Pomeroy

   ix. Japhet, baptized 15 October 1642, Roxbury, Massachusetts

   x. Hannah, born 2 December 1644, Springfield, Massachusetts

Although this is a typical genealogical account, it leaves out some very important details. What was Cicely like? How did she dress? What did she eat? What was her daily life like? Obviously, if the woman lived to be more than eighty years old, she did more than get married, have babies and die. But based on this summary, one would think that this is *all* she did and all she needed to be remembered for. I disagree.

The first step in reconstructing her life is to learn as much about Cicely as possible from genealogical sources, which give the details of her family. To open the door for social history research, formulate some questions about her life. In other words, what would you want to know about Cicely? If she were sitting before you, what questions would you ask her about her life?

One of the areas that interested me was how she might have dressed. From elementary school days, I had grown up with a stereotypical image of colonial New England women: They all dressed in black or gray dresses that had white cuffs and collars, and they all wore white aprons and caps. Was that how it really was?

In searching the genealogical records, I found an inventory of Cicely's possessions taken after her death.[10] It revealed some interesting clothing items:

> One pr of Bodyes, a *green* apron & a Wascoate . . . a Cloak & Cloath hood
> One Cloath Wascoate & one serge Wascoate . . . *blue* apron, serge Neckcloath
> 4 coats . . . a Cloath hood . . . one pr stockings, 2 Wascoats

Green and blue aprons? Although I don't know the color of the rest of the garments, I discovered that she didn't wear white aprons as I had thought. Was this typical? And why green and blue? I then turned my research to social histories like the ones in the Bibliography to learn more about whether owning green and blue aprons was common or whether Cicely was some sort of seventeenth-century fashion trendsetter.

In books such as David Hackett Fischer's *Albion's Seed: Four British Folkways in America*, George Dow's *Every Day Life in the Massachusetts Bay Colony* and Alice Morse Earle's *Customs and Fashions in Old New England*, I checked the index under the following topics: "dress," "clothing," "sewing," "fashion" and "costume." Through this research, I discovered that colonial New Englanders liked what they called "sad" colors: greens, blues, purples, oranges and so forth. Taking notes on what I found, I was able to summarize:

> The people of colonial New England did not dress in black, gray and white as stereotypical sketches in school textbooks portray. They preferred what they called "sad" colors, such as green, blue, purple and orange. Black was generally avoided and reserved for the ruling elders. The style of clothing was governed by the colony lawmakers, who deemed it illegal to wear short sleeves; gold, silver, and silk lace; and more than one slash on the sleeve. (A slash in the sleeve allowed for fabric of another color to show through.) Clothing was a durable item that was passed down to the next generation.

Using this same paragraph, I inserted the genealogical information I knew about Cicely:

> Cicely owned many articles of clothing: a pair of bodyes, green and blue aprons, a neckcloath, five was-coates, a pair of stockings, four coats, a cloak and two cloath hoods. While it is not known what colors her clothing were, the inventory of her estate reveals green and blue aprons.[11] The people of colonial New England did not dress in black, gray and white as stereotypical sketches in school textbooks portray. They preferred what they called "sad" colors, such as green, blue, purple and orange. Black was generally avoided and reserved for the ruling elders. The style of clothing was governed by the colony lawmakers, who deemed it illegal to wear short sleeves; gold, silver, and silk lace; and more than one slash on the sleeve. (A slash in the sleeve allowed for fabric of another color to show through.) Clothing was a durable item that was passed down to the next generation.[12]

Even if I had not had an inventory for Cicely and had not known what color her aprons were, I could still use the information:

> The people of colonial New England did not dress in black, gray and white as stereotypical sketches in school textbooks portray. They preferred what they called "sad" colors, such as green, blue, purple and orange. Black was generally avoided and reserved for the ruling elders. The style of clothing was governed by the colony lawmakers, who deemed it illegal to wear short sleeves; gold,

silver, and silk lace; and more than one slash on the sleeve. (A slash in the sleeve allowed for fabric of another color to show through.) Clothing was a durable item that was passed down to the next generation. While it is not known what colors Cicely Penny's dresses and aprons were, she, too, probably wore dresses of these various colors.

What did Cicely eat? Consulting the same sources and Laurel Thatcher Ulrich's *Good Wives: Image and Reality in the Lives of Women in Northern New England, 1650–1750*, I learned that women would have eaten and prepared their food in America as they and their mothers had done in England. An important staple was pease porridge. In Cicely's day peas were baked or boiled. Most people ate peas, hot or cold, three times a day. Even though I don't have any genealogical records to tell me if this is what she ate, I can speculate that she probably ate pease porridge sometime in her life:

Although no food or spices were listed in Samuel or Cicely Chapin's inventories,[13] probates of other New England families suggest what the Chapins probably ate. Peas or beans were a main staple in the New Englander's diet. Peas were baked or boiled, and most people ate them hot or cold, three times a day. Along with this porridge, they consumed loaves of a coarse, dark brown bread made from wheat or rye flour and cornmeal. With their meals, the common bever-

age was English beer or ale. Vegetables such as parsnips, turnips, onions and cabbage also graced their tables, as well as game meats. Perhaps it was the colonial New Englander's diet—low in fat and rich in protein, fiber and carbohydrates[14]—that contributed to Samuel and Cicely's long lives. He was about seventy-seven when he died in 1675, and she was eighty-one at her death in 1682.[15]

Just by isolating a few aspects of your female ancestor's life, then researching in social histories what was typical or common for ordinary people, you can easily supplement your genealogical information—or lack thereof—and write a short biography of your female ancestor.

Let's look at another example.

Caroline: A Slave Woman in Virginia

Here is a summary of what is known about Caroline:[16]

Caroline———, living in Virginia in 1844. Owned by James Madison Fitzhugh of Orange County, Virginia.

Children:
  i. Mary
  ii. Martha
  iii. George
  iv. Susan

Sadly, in terms of genealogical research, Caroline is insignificant. She was a slave, had no rights and owned nothing. Without plantation records, there is no way of knowing who the father of her children were. It could have been another slave (who might also be her husband), who lived either on the same plantation with Caroline or at a neighboring one. The father of some of her children might also be her master. We don't know whether she had other children besides these four. We don't know her age, where she was born or who her parents were. We don't know when she died: before or after emancipation. Everything that is known about her has come from one record: a deed of her and her children's legal transfer to James's wife in January 1844.[17] Some information about her may be handed down through oral history, but at this point, I'm not aware of any. Though further research may reveal other records that name her and her children, this is likely all I will have to work with.

So how would you write a biography of her life? Or is she one of the ones who is doomed to be silent? Remember in the Introduction I said that *every* woman led a life worth researching and recording? Caroline's life is no less significant than anyone else's. Her story deserves to be told, too. This is where social histories are so valuable. When you have a woman in your ancestry who did not create any records and had very few created about her, then you need to supplement with social histories and speculate on what her life was *probably* like, based on women's lives like your ancestor's.

Again, ask yourself what aspects of Caroline's life you would like to know about. Perhaps you want to know what a typical day in her life on the plantation was

like. If so, look for books that discuss this topic. You might begin with a general women's history, such as Evans's *Born for Liberty: A History of Women in America*. In the index, look under "slave women—work." Also check that author's sources of information to lead you to other sources more specific to your topic, such as Jacqueline Jones's *Labor of Love, Labor of Sorrow: Black Women, Work, and the Family From Slavery to the Present*. Once you have an idea of what slave women typically did on a daily basis, you can summarize the social history:

> Most slave women worked the fields, toiling for fourteen hours a day under the hot sun. Field work required quite a bit of strength to plant, hoe and harvest the crops. Even if pregnant, they worked the fields up until the last month of pregnancy and returned to work a month after the birth. At the end of the day, slave women were not idle. At night and on Sundays, they needed to tend to their families. Many slave women were allowed to grow vegetables in their own gardens, which supplemented their families' diets. They also prepared their families' meals, cared for their children, washed clothes and attended to other housekeeping chores.

Now let's use this paragraph and insert Caroline and her children:

> Though it is not known whether Caroline was a house or field slave for

the Fitzhugh family of Orange County, Virginia, most slave women on small plantations worked the fields, and Caroline probably did, too. As a field slave, Caroline would toil for fourteen hours a day under the hot sun. Field work required quite a bit of strength to plant, hoe and harvest the crops. Even when Caroline was pregnant, she would have worked the fields up until the last month of pregnancy and returned to work a month after the birth. At the end of the day, slave women like Caroline were not idle. At night and on Sundays, she needed to tend to her family. Caroline was probably allowed to grow vegetables in her own garden, which supplemented her family's diet. She also prepared her family's meals, cared for her children—Mary, Martha, George and Susan—washed their clothes and attended to other housekeeping chores.[18]

Though I have no documents or family stories to tell me what Caroline's daily life was like, I can speculate based on what other slave women did on a daily basis. In an introduction or in notes, you can inform the reader that you are speculating, citing the social histories as your sources. The opening remarks alone clue the reader that you have no specific documentation about Caroline's life: "Though it is not known . . . and Caroline probably did, too."

In your research and writing, you can focus on any aspect of a woman's life that piques your curiosity. Then research the social history—the typical experience. Blend it with what you know about your ancestor and write her story.

Let's look at one more example that deals with an immigrant woman during the early twentieth century.

Anna (———) Banoni: An Urban Immigrant Woman

Anna is another woman who gives researchers trouble in locating information specifically about her:[19]

> Anna——— was born in October 1865 in Italy and died by 1925 in New York City. She married Giuseppe Banoni about 1880, probably in Italy. He was born in October 1851 in Italy and died about 1936 in New York City. They immigrated to America between 1882 and 1885.

Children:
  i. Michele, born March 1881, Italy
       >5 year gap
  ii. Giuseppe, born February 1886, New York
       >almost 5 year gap
  iii. Francesca, born October 1890, New York
       >3 year gap
  iv. Antonio, born October 1893, New York
       >5 year gap
  v. Salvatore, born November 1898, New York

Anna's family is a typical, poor, immigrant family living in a large city. They did not own a home in New York City but lived in a tenement apartment, so there are no land records. Anna died before her husband and left no will. The only information about her came from census records, which state that she was the mother of five children, with five living. The gaps in the birth of her children are the part of her life that fascinated me. Why are there so many gaps, and why are they somewhat consistently spaced? Could this woman be practicing birth control?

Turning to social history research, you could begin with books like Doris Weatherford's *Foreign and Female: Immigrant Women in America, 1840–1930* and Elizabeth Ewen's *Immigrant Women in the Land of Dollars*. Look in the index under family size, birth control, contraceptives or abortion.

The social historians here did not rely on women's letters and diaries because most immigrant women were either illiterate and did not leave accounts, or could write but did not record intimate topics. Intimate matters about sex and birth control were generally handed down orally from mother to daughter. So these historians focused their studies on oral history interviews. From their research, Weatherford and Ewen explained that immigrant women living in urban areas at the turn of the twentieth century were beginning to practice family planning by using birth control. The historians reported that one of the most common forms of contraception for poor immigrant women at that time was self-inflicted or aided abortions. Another was sleeping apart from their husbands. I also consulted books specific to Italian American culture that also discussed this topic.

Now let's probe deeper into the history of birth control and abortion, in books such as John D'Emilio and Estelle B. Freedman's *Intimate Matters: A History of Sexuality in America* and James C. Mohr's *Abortion in America: The Origins and Evolution of National Policy, 1800–1900.* These authors concurred that abortion was common in America and did not carry the stigma it does today. Based on the information in the social histories, let's speculate on those gaps in the births of Anna's children:

Anna Banoni was the mother of only five children, all of whom survived to adulthood. Interestingly, between the births of her children, there are three five-year gaps and one three-year gap.[20] While it was typical for children to be naturally spaced apart by about two years, these longer intervals could be the result of miscarriage, stillbirths or difficulties in conceiving. A more likely explanation, however, was that Anna was deliberately limiting her family size. The birth intervals are not sporadic as would have been the case if the reasons were miscarriage, stillbirths or problems with conception. Instead, the gaps are at fairly uniform lengths. The use of birth control (sleeping apart from her husband) and particularly the practice of self-inflicted or aided abortions, were common among immigrant and especially Italian women who lived in the late-nineteenth-century ethnic enclaves of New York City.[21] It is likely that Anna deliberately controlled the size of her family by using one or both of these methods.

Since we are dealing with intimate and controversial topics such as birth control and abortion, it would be a good idea to follow this paragraph with an explanation that supports your speculation. For example, further reading about immigrant women would tell you that in the Old Country, the family's main form of income was from agriculture. A large family was needed to work the fields. Once in America, large families were crowded into two-room tenement apartments. Men now worked as day laborers. A large family was no longer necessary or desired. More children meant more mouths to feed.

Not only does the social history augment your family history, it can also explain family skeletons and information you find during the course of your genealogical research. Remember Harriet (Symonds) Easton from chapter two? She was the one who died at age twenty-seven in 1850 from an abortion, but neither her cause of death nor the birth and death of her three-week-old daughter were included in the published family history. Though the author in 1899 may have considered an abortion a skeleton (or he simply did not know her cause of death), a genealogist today could

handle the sensitive material in the following manner:

Twenty-six-year-old Harriet Symonds married forty-two-year-old widower Agis Easton in September 1848. She became the stepmother to his five children born to his first wife. A year after Harriet's wedding, she gave birth to a baby girl, whom she named after herself. The infant lived only three weeks, however. Less than six months later, Harriet was pregnant again. Exhausted, and probably distraught by the loss of her first child, Harriet sought an abortion. Though it is not known whether she was aided by a midwife or friend in helping her to terminate the pregnancy, or if she tried to abort by herself, it resulted in her death in March 1850.

In this paragraph we have given her a possible motivation for her actions. Whether or not we agree with her decision, she certainly must have had her reasons. Being distraught over the recent loss of one baby and having five other stepchildren to raise in the household were likely catalysts.

Documenting Your Ancestor's History

As you write the story of your women ancestors' lives, remember that an important and vital part of genealogy and family history is *documentation*—citing your sources of information. You must note in which record or book you found a particular date, place or an ancestor's name and parents. Today's genealogists want to know that their ancestries are accurate. How did you come to the conclusion that Wifflehoffer is Matilda's maiden name? It is not enough just to say so. What's your proof? What record gave you that information? How do you (and we) know this is the right name? How do you (and we) know that this doesn't lead us on a chase for the wrong ancestors?

Citing your sources is not optional when you write a family history. It is important to tell your readers and descendants (in endnotes or footnotes) where all of the genealogical and historical information has come from.

As you can see from the examples in this chapter, writing your female ancestor's biography is really rather simple if you supplement your genealogical research with information from social histories. A woman no longer has to be immortalized only for the day she was born, the day she married, the day she gave birth and the day she died. Her life had a great deal of substance. It's up to you to seek it out and write about it. Don't you think her life is worth the effort to make her legacy more than just a name on a chart or a piece of paper? In the next chapter, you'll see how all the ingredients come together for the final step in the recipe for researching and writing about your female ancestors.

CHAPTER SIX

From Start to Finish: A Case Study of Mary Fitzhugh (Stuart) Fitzhugh

Women will starve in silence until new stories are created which confer on them the power of naming themselves.

Sandra Gilbert and Susan Gubar,
as quoted in Carolyn G. Heilbrun's,
Writing a Woman's Life

Throughout this book, I've presented methods and sources for researching your female ancestors. Then I showed you brief examples of how to blend social history research with family history to write a narrative about your female ancestors. Now it's time to put it all together. Without a literary example to follow, it may be difficult to envision how the ingredients become a whole. Questions about writing biographies abound: Does the narrative have to start with the day a woman was born? What should her biography look like? What parts of her life should be included and what parts can be left out? As Carolyn G. Heilbrun points out in *Writing a Woman's Life*, "What matters is that lives do not serve as models; only stories do that. . . . We can only retell and live by the stories we have read or heard. . . . Whatever their form or medium, these stories have formed us all; they are what we must use to make . . . new narratives."

To give you a narrative example to follow, let me walk you through the steps of taking a woman from a name on a chart to a finished biographical narrative.

Home Sources

On my pedigree chart, I had a woman named Mary Fitzhugh (Stuart) Fitzhugh, who was my third great grandmother. My great aunts had supplied me with basic information about her that someone else in the family had compiled, such as her approximate birth and death dates and places. I also made contact with another Fitzhugh descendant who supplied me with Mary's obituary from the *Washington Star* (Albemarle County, Virginia) newspaper. It revealed the following information:

Fitzhugh, died on August 31, 1881, at the residence of her son-in-law, Mr. T.A. Marshall, near Lindsay's, Albemarle Co., Va. Mrs. Mary Stuart Fitzhugh, relict of James Madison Fitzhugh, and daughter of David Stuart of King George County, Va., age seventy-one years.

She had been a member of the

Episcopal Church since 1831 and having served her Lord for half a century, death possessed no terrors for her, but was looked upon and awaited calmly and patiently as a translation to a better and brighter world, as a means of being reunited to her husband and children who had preceded her. . . .

So when the summons came it found her calm, peaceful, self-possessed, and hopeful, relying upon the Savior in whom she had trusted, and though at intervals suffering the most agonizing pain, her constant prayer was "Lord, take thy servant to thyself." No murmur, no petition for relief from pain, no request for recovery to health, simply, "Lord, take me home."

In so brief a notice we cannot dwell upon the virtues of the deceased lady. In all the relations of life, as a wife, mother, friend and neighbor she endeavored to fulfill her duty, and her sweet patience and resignation under trials, the most severe loss of husband and children, reverses of fortune, and years of physical suffering endeared her to all who knew her. Her consideration for others was such that even on her death bed she expressed herself as being glad that her children were not there to witness her suffering.

Thanking those around her for their unwearied attention, she said, "My time has come to die; this is my last day upon earth; but I do not fear death. I am ready and willing to go." Then she tried to sing a hymn which her husband had sung when dying, "There is room in Paradise for me," and beckoned to some celestial visitant invisible to our mortal sight, but hovering probably above her ready to waft her spirit across the dark river to realms of perpetual bliss. . . .

Published Genealogical Sources

Genealogists usually check to see if someone else has published a family history on their ancestors before embarking on original research. Volume two of *Genealogies of Virginia Families From the Virginia Magazine of History and Biography* confirmed the dates and places my aunts had given me for Mary. This source also gave information on her children:

Mary Fitzhugh Stuart, daughter of David and Charlotte Hawes (Buckner) Stuart, was born about 1810 in King George County, Virginia; died 31 August 1881, Albemarle County, Virginia; married 19 July 1830, to James Madison Fitzhugh. James, son of Henry and Elizabeth (Conway) Fitzhugh, was born 25 April 1809, Virginia; died 20 February 1845, Orange County, Virginia.

Children:
   i. Catlett Conway, b. 25 Apr 1831, King George Co., Virginia
   ii. John Stuart, b. ca. 1835, Virginia
   iii. Battaile, b. ca. 1837, Virginia

iv. Francis Conway, b. 12 Aug 1839,
   Orange Co., Virginia

v. Louisa Conway, b. ca. 1841,
   Orange Co., Virginia

vi. Oscar Stuart, b. 22 July 1842,
   Virginia

vii. James Madison, b. ca. 1844,
   Virginia

Research began by focusing on Mary, so the next step was to find marriage and death records for her. Death records were not routinely filed in Virginia until after 1912, so it is not surprising that there was no death certificate for Mary. The Family History Library in Salt Lake City, Utah, has marriage records on microfilm from the courthouse in King George County, Virginia. It confirmed the date of her marriage to James: 19 July 1830.

Population Schedules

Turning to census records, the family of James Madison Fitzhugh was enumerated in 1840 in Greene County, Virginia:

	[ages]	
free males	0–5	2 (probably sons Francis and Battaile)
	5–10	1 (probably son John)
	10–15	1 (probably son Catlett)
	30–40	1 (probably head of household, James M.)
free females	0–5	1 (probably daughter Louisa who was born about 1841)
	20–30	1 (Mary was about 30 in 1840, so she could be enumerated in this category or the following.)
	30–40	1
	40–50	1 (The other two females in the household are unknown.)
slave males	0–10	1
	10–24	2
	24–36	1
	36–55	1
	55–100	1
slave females	0–10	5
	10–24	1
	24–36	1
	36–52	1

By 1850, Mary had become a widow and was the head of the household. She was living in Orange County, Virginia, with her children: John, Francis, Louisa, Oscar and James M. Son Battaile is not listed, indicating that he may have died before 1850. Mary was easily followed in the 1860 and 1870 censuses for Orange County (she hasn't been found in 1880). From the census records, I learned about Mary's household: She owned land and slaves. This led to deeds and slave censuses, as well as a search for her husband's will.

Probate and Court Records

James Madison Fitzhugh did leave a will. It was dated 8 May 1844 and was recorded 24 March 1845 in Orange County, Virginia. He bequeathed his whole estate, real and personal, to his wife, Mary F. Fitzhugh. He also gave her the power to dispose of any of his property that she thought best, provided she did not marry. She now became a *feme sole*. James stipulated in his will that if she did remarry, she would forfeit all of James's property, in which case it was to be equally divided among his children (whom he does not name). This was James's way of ensuring that his property would stay in his family line and not become part of a future husband's estate. James further stated in his will, however, "If my wife should marry and demand her thirds, at her death, this portion of my estate I desire to be equally divided between my children forever." James was acknowledging that, by law, Mary was entitled to her dower regardless, but it was only a life-interest third (for the term of her life), then it would go to his children instead of any children Mary might have by a second marriage. He also named Mary as his executrix. Besides not naming his children, he also did not name the fourteen slaves he would have also bequeathed as a part of his property.

Before we look at records of Mary's life after James's death, such as the slave and agricultural censuses, let's look for land records. In the indexes for King George and Orange counties in Virginia, there are a number of transactions involving James Madison Fitzhugh and his wife, Mary. One, however, is particularly interesting. It is a deed dated 29 January 1844, the same year James made out his will:

This Indenture made this 29th day of January in the year of our Lord one thousand eight hundred and forty four, between James M Fitzhugh of the first part, James B Newman of the second part and Mary F Fitzhugh of the third part all of the County of Orange and State of Virginia. . . . whereas the said James M Fitzhugh for . . . natural love and affection for his said wife and children is willing and desirous of settling the following slaves upon his said wife, and their children now living, or that may hereafter be born to them viz: a negro woman Caroline and her four children Mary, Martha, George and Susan; Anna and her five children, John Willis, Fanny, Lucy Ann, Gibbons and Leverine; Adeline and her child Sarah Ann, Harriett and her children Lot, Julia and Samuel, a negro man Ely and all the future increase of the females thereof, by conveying them to the said James B Newman in trust for that purpose. . . .

James must have been ill and known he was going to die soon, so he transferred his slaves over to his wife, to be held in trust by James B. Newman. James Newman was Fitzhugh's brother-in-law, married to his sister, Sarah. Although we still have no document naming James Fitzhugh's children, we now know the names of his slaves:

Caroline and four children: Mary, Martha, George and Susan
Anna and five children: John Willis, Fanny, Lucy Ann, Gibbons and Leverine

Adeline and her child: Sarah Ann
Harriett and three children: Lot, Julia
    and Samuel
Ely

According to this document, there are now eighteen slaves.

Slave Schedules

Now let's look at slave schedules. In Orange County in 1850, five years after James's death, Mary is listed with only ten slaves:

female	age 49	mulatto
female	age 40	mulatto
male	age 8	mulatto [born 1841–2]
male	age 6	mulatto [born 1843–4]
male	age 4	mulatto [born 1846]
female	age 24	mulatto
female	age 7	mulatto [born 1843]
female	age 4	mulatto [born 1846]
male	age 1	mulatto [born 1849]
male	age 35	black

Either Mary has sold eight slaves, or some may have died. Ely may be the thirty-five-year-old black slave. There are three adult women; but James named four female slaves with children. Some of the children listed here would not have been born when James conveyed his slaves to Mary. The female, age twenty-four, may be Adeline, whose daughter Sarah Ann would have been alive in 1844. The other female and male were born after 1844. Caroline, Anna and Harriett all had several children, so it is difficult to determine who the other two adult females were. As the children reached adolescence, they may have been sold.

The 1860 Orange County, Virginia, slave schedule for Mary showed just eight slaves right before the outbreak of the Civil War:

male	age 18	black
male	age 6	black
female	age 62	black
female	age 21	black
female	age 18	black
female	age 14	black
female	age 9	black
female	age 9	black

After the war, on the 1870 Orange County, Virginia, population census, Mary's neighbors are now free black families working as farmhands. This is how that census looked:

Carter,

William	25	male	black	farm hand
Milly	22	female	black	keeps house
Rose	3	female	black	at home

Watson,

Martha	12	female	black	nurse

Wright,

Edward	23	male	black	farm hand
Thomas	13	male	black	farm hand

Fitzhugh,

John S.	35	male	white	farm hand
Mary F.	60	female	white	keeps house

Taylor,

Joseph	50	male	black	farm hand
Eliza	55	female	black	keeps house
William	21	male	black	farm hand
Jacob	18	male	black	farm hand
Charles	14	male	black	farm hand

Along with these documents, other records on Mary and her family were abundant:

tax lists, agricultural schedules and court records. Genealogically speaking, she is a gold mine of information, mainly because she became and remained a widow. Yet none of the records told me much about her as a person. In particular, how did she cope with being a thirty-five-year-old widow with six children? She also had a plantation of about 420 acres with a dozen or so slaves. From the records above, we know that her brother-in-law James B. Newman must have given her guidance, since her husband had placed so much trust in him. What was her life like? Mary never remarried, and during the Civil War, at least three of her sons served in the Confederacy. How did she handle all that? If Mary left any letters or diaries, they either no longer exist or are buried in someone's attic and long forgotten.

Social History Research

After gathering a multitude of records on Mary and her family, it was time to turn to social histories to augment the genealogical information. (All of the books mentioned are in the Bibliography.) I began with general histories of women to get an overview. In the following books, I read information specific to Southern plantation women and their slaves:

> Sara M. Evans's *Born for Liberty: A History of Women in America*
> Carol Hymowitz and Michaele Weissman's *A History of Women in America*

Then I focused on plantation and Southern women, about which much has been written. Here are a few of the sources I researched:

> Carol Bleser's *In Joy and in Sorrow: Women, Family, and Marriage in the Victorian South, 1830–1900*
> Catherine Clinton's *The Plantation Mistress: Woman's World in the Old South*
> Catherine Clinton and Nina Silber's *Divided Houses: Gender and the Civil War*
> Elizabeth Fox-Genovese's *Within the Plantation Household: Black and White Women of the Old South*

Some of the books I read cover to cover; others I perused for specific information. As I read these books, I took notes on topics, circumstances and experiences of which Mary would have likely been a part. For example, after Mary was left a widow, she no doubt relied upon her oldest sons to help her manage the plantation. These social history sources confirmed that Southern sons were devoted to their widowed mothers. They and other male relatives would have given her legal and economic guidance when they reached adulthood. Other topics I learned about that interested me were white-black relations, drug addiction, women's rights, daily responsibilities and the roles of Southern wives and mothers. A few of these topics intrigued me to the point of seeking out sources specific on them, such as drug addiction, leading me to David T. Courtwright's *Dark Paradise: Opiate Addiction in America Before 1940*.

I also religiously read the authors' notes

and bibliographies. Notes are sometimes more comprehensive than the bibliography and may discuss the strengths and weaknesses of a source. In the notes and "bib," I find different and unusual social histories, and sometimes original sources to seek; in finding these, I usually discover even more sources. It's a fascinating chain reaction.

Reading social histories not only gave me material with which to write a biography of Mary, but they also helped me to "connect" with her. Though it shocked me at first to think that my third great-grandmother could have been an opium addict or could have had illicit relations with a slave, through my readings, I was able to gain an understanding of women like her and to empathize with her circumstances. Mary led an interesting life, with obstacles and struggles that would have been a challenge for many women of her day. Although a slave owner, Mary was also a victim of slavery. Social histories reveal that many Southern women of Mary's time and station felt slavery was a moral evil, yet they were forced to accept it. I gained a great deal of respect and admiration for my foremother through my research on her. She was and forever will be more than just a name on a chart.

Reading Mary Fitzhugh's Biography
As you read the following biography about Mary, study each paragraph and its corresponding endnotes. Try to separate in your mind the social history from the family history. Then look at how the two are blended together. Notice, too, that I've used the "flashback" technique common in writing fiction.

The narrative begins with the year Mary became a widow—probably one of the most significant times of her life. As with any type of writing, it is important to grab the reader's attention in the first paragraph, so try to pick the most interesting or significant aspect of a woman's life to begin the story. You will also notice that I did not use every single fact I had learned about Mary. I used only the information that was relevant to the theme of the biography: her life as a widow.

In her biography, the introductory paragraph is followed by discussion on the lack of some sources and the methods used to augment the sources I did find. Then I come back to Mary's story, and it is told in more of a chronological order. You will also notice that I speculate about topics relevant to Mary's life, such as drug addiction and illicit sex. I have no concrete evidence that Mary engaged in either of these activities; yet these were typical experiences for women like Mary. Though it may shock some readers (and probably my cousins!), the social history evidence is strong enough to include the speculation. It also dispels the myth that Southern plantation women sat on the veranda all day long drinking mint juleps!

This is not meant to be a book in itself; research on Mary and her family is ongoing. It focuses on selected topics that interested me or on which I had genealogical documents to connect with the social history. The goal of this biography is to give readers (her descendants) an appreciation for this woman and her life.

An Antebellum Widow's Struggle: Mary Fitzhugh (Stuart) Fitzhugh of Virginia

The year Mary Fitzhugh (Stuart) Fitzhugh turned thirty-five was the year she learned what life as a single mother would be like. Born in King George County, Virginia, about 1810,[1] at twenty she married[2] into the prominent and influential Fitzhugh family, which had resided in Virginia since the early 1600s.[3] Mary was the daughter of David and Charlotte Hawes (Buckner) Stuart, another prominent family in Caroline and King George counties, Virginia.[4] Nine months after Mary married James Madison Fitzhugh, she gave birth to their first child, Catlett Conway, and during the next fifteen years she bore six more children: John Stuart, born in 1835; Battaile, born in 1837; Francis Conway, born in 1839; Louisa Conway, born in 1841; Oscar Stuart, born in 1842; and James Madison, born in 1844.[5] Even more children would have probably followed had it not been for her husband's early death at age thirty-six.[6] Living on a small plantation of about 420 acres, Mary was now alone to raise her children, ages one to fourteen, and to manage a dozen slaves and the plantation.[7]

Although no letters, diaries or plantation account books are known to have survived for Mary, enough bureaucratic documents—censuses (population, slave, agricultural), tax records (land and personal property), deeds and court cases—have survived to allow a glimpse into her life before and after she became a widow. Though these records help to piece together the sterile facts of her

circumstances, none tell how she might have coped as a young widow. Thus, in order to speculate about this aspect of her life, a look into the lives of women like Mary in similar circumstances is necessary.

Scholarship on women who remained widows in the antebellum South, however, is scarce—probably because most widows remarried out of economic necessity within a few years of their husbands' passing. Few were as determined and progressive as Mary must have been to stay a widow and to run her own plantation. In this instance, then, where there is a lack of relevant material on a specific subject, research took an alternative path and focused on women who were left alone to manage the homefront during the Civil War while their husbands were off serving the Confederacy. This circumstance would have most closely matched the hardships Mary would have encountered as a widow in 1845.

As was common for a Southern woman raised in the planter society of Virginia, Mary married her second cousin, James Madison Fitzhugh, in 1830, when she was twenty.[8] Like all white Southern females of her day, Mary had been raised from birth for her ultimate duty as a wife and mother. Marital arrangements between cousins served two purposes in the planter class. It was a means to tighten the family circle, keeping the wealth distributed among the family; and many women preferred to marry a cousin with whom they were familiar rather than a stranger. After marriage, Mary was expected to leave her father's home and move to wherever her husband chose to live. Her life thereafter was confined to a domestic world on her husband's plantation.[9]

The life of a plantation mistress in the antebellum South was not one of leisure and luxury. She generally worked as hard as her slaves. Besides managing the household finances, Mary would have had numerous tasks that occupied her time. She gardened; salted pork; made candles, soap, linens and clothing; preserved fruits and vegetables; and cared for the slaves. While she probably did not do the cooking or washing herself, she did supervise these chores performed by house slaves. One ongoing project for Mary would have been knitting socks for her "family, white and black":[10]

> A stocking took 185 stitches per row, on the average, and most plantation mistresses could manage to fit in 150 rows per day. . . . A single sock took six days; [so] a housewife could complete a pair of stockings every two weeks.[11]

Along with her daily activities about the plantation, child raising fell upon Mary's shoulders, but she also delegated many of the mundane tasks to her household slaves. Mary would have done the disciplining and educating of her children until the boys were ready to be sent to school. Her daughter, Louisa, stayed on the plantation with Mary, repeating the cycle and preparing for her future role as a devoted wife and mother.[12]

Though Mary was subordinate to her husband in all respects, during his absence everyone answered to her as the plantation mistress. Slaves and the overseer, however, recognized that she acted merely as her husband's delegate, never fully having control in running the plantation.[13]

In 1840, five years before Mary's husband died, the census enumerator reported the composition of the household:[14]

	[ages]	
free males	0–5	2 (probably sons Francis and Battaile)
	5–10	1 (probably son John)
	15–20	1 (probably son Catlett)
	30–40	1 (probably head of household, James M.)
free females	0–5	1 (probably daughter Louisa who was born about 1841)
	20–30	1 (Mary was about 30 in 1840, so she could be enumerated in this category or the following.)
	30–40	1
	40–50	1 (The other two females in the household are unknown.)
slave males	0–10	1
	10–24	2
	24–36	1
	36–55	1
	55 100	1
slave females	0–10	5
	10–24	1
	24–36	1
	36–52	1

The Fitzhugh household can be classified as a conventional, small planter unit with fourteen slaves, as opposed to large plantations whose owners held more than twenty slaves, and yeomen farmers who owned nine or less. Slavery was an accepted way of life for women of the antebellum South, like Mary. Whether she agreed with human bondage or not, the majority of women realized that the Southern economy was dependent on slave labor.[15]

One aspect of slavery that women did not like but were forced to tolerate, however, was if their husbands engaged in sexual relations with slave women. Male planters rationalized their intimate liaisons as an economic solution to replenishing slave labor. Importation of human cargo was no longer legal by the time James and Mary married, making it more difficult to acquire new slaves. In order to increase the slave population, slaves were forced to mate with each other and with the white slaveholder, if he so desired. Not surprisingly, no personal documents, public records or oral traditions exist to confirm whether Mary's husband had relations with his slaves. This was a matter discussed mainly behind closed doors with other slave owners; it became public knowledge in some court cases or with the birth of light-colored slaves who resembled their owner. The incidence of slaveholders engaging in sexual relations with their slaves was common enough, however, to speculate that James likely had sex with a slave at some point in his life—either as an adolescent on his father's plantation or while he was married and owned his own human chattel.[16]

As already has been seen in the 1840 enumeration, James owned fourteen slaves, with at least two or more males in their reproductive prime. This census does not indicate, however, whether the slaves were black or mulatto. A comparison with the slave schedule for 1850 shows that of the ten slaves listed, only one is black, a thirty-five-year-old male. The rest were recorded as mulatto.[17] The slaves denoted with asterisks in 1840 could possibly be the same slaves listed ten years later in 1850:

1840

slave males	0–10	1
	10–24	2
	24–36	1*
	36–55	1
	55–100	1
slave females	0–10	5
	10–24	1*
	24–36	1*
	36–52	1*

1850

female	age 49	mulatto*
female	age 40	mulatto*
male	age 8	mulatto
male	age 6	mulatto
male	age 4	mulatto
female	age 24	mulatto*
female	age 7	mulatto
female	age 4	mulatto
male	age 1	mulatto
male	age 35	black*

In accounting for the whereabouts of the other slaves between 1840 and 1850, some may have died and the adolescent ones sold. Given that six were under the age of ten, and two were between thirty-six and one hundred years of age, these slaves were likely lost to disease or old age. While these slaves passed on, new chattel joined the household: six mulatto babies were born during this ten-year span.

Five months before James made his will in May 1844, he conveyed eighteen slaves to his wife, Mary, out of "natural love and affection": Caroline and four children: Mary, Martha, George and Susan; Anna and five children: John Willis, Fanny, Lucy Ann, Gibbons and Leverine; Adeline and her child: Sarah Ann; Harriett and her three children: Lot, Julia and Samuel; and a Negro man named Ely. James B. Newman, Fitzhugh's brother-in-law by marriage to his sister Sarah, was given the trust of overseeing the property for Mary.[18]

When James died the following year, he bequeathed to Mary his entire estate, real and personal, and everything that he possessed, granting her the power to dispose of any of his property as she thought best, provided, however, that Mary "does not marry a second time—In that event, [his] desire is that her fee simple right to all of [his] property be forfeited. . . ."[19] Under the law, Mary now became a *feme sole*, which meant that as long as she remained a widow, she had many of the same legal rights as a man. She could make land transactions and run her plantation as she chose. If she married again, she lost all of the property, unless she demanded her widow's thirds. Mary, though no doubt saddened by her husband's demise, probably came to enjoy her independence. For this reason and probably others—perhaps loyalty, respect, love or a combination of these—Mary chose to remain a widow, facing the challenges and rewards her new status brought.

Mary probably sought the advice and representation of her brother-in-law James Newman or other relatives until she felt confident in running her affairs herself. Southern sons were particularly devoted to their mothers in such circumstances. A widow's sons, as well as other male relatives such as her brothers, were expected to help her with financial needs. They provided her with the legal and economic guidance necessary for her to survive as a planter.[20]

Mary's sons appear to have been loyal to the responsibility that Southern society expected of them. Five years after James's death, Mary no doubt relied on her fifteen-year-old son, John, since her eldest son was no longer living with the family. In 1860, Mary's household consisted of just herself, her eighteen-year-old son, Oscar, and ten slaves. By 1870, son John resumed his role as his mother's caretaker—at age thirty-five, he and his sixty-year-old mother lived together in Orange County, Virginia.[21]

A fifteen-year-old and even an eighteen-year-old son, however, would not have provided Mary with all the guidance that managing a slaveholding plantation required. No doubt she also relied on the services of a white male overseer who lived nearby. One overseer, by the name of George Kerlby, lived two dwellings away from the Fitzhugh plantation in 1860, making him a possible candidate for the position.[22]

Like other women in her class, Mary's world consisted of her home; society did not allow her to venture to neighboring plantations or towns without male guidance. Essentially isolated on the plantation, five years after James died she and her nine-year-old daughter Louisa were the only white women on the estate.[23] Depression and loneliness plagued widows, and Mary had to have been bothered by these emotions, too. Some women turned to laudanum to relieve their depression. Mary's life fits the profile of a typical drug addict of the nineteenth century: a middle-aged, widowed, Southern plantation owner. Many patent medicines and home remedies had opiates or alcohol as a base. It was common for women of Mary's station to become addicted to opium, morphine and alcohol. Women like Mary also sought solace in their religion or in their children's lives. But, even though widows were surrounded by their families, white and black, they were lonely for their mates—after all, women like Mary were raised with one goal in mind: to be a companion to their husbands. How was it then, that Mary survived the loneliness of thirty-six years of widowhood until she died at age seventy-one?[24]

Some widows, out of desperate loneliness, threw all caution to the wind and engaged in a taboo relationship with one of their male slaves. Historians writing on the subject of black-white relationships in the antebellum South have been able to document through personal papers, court records and the lighter-colored mulatto children born to slave women that white men commonly consorted with black female slaves. Cases of white women having sexual relations with their black slaves, on the other hand, have left "an intriguing historical silence [that] masks their frequency and dynamics."[25] One historian, however, has been able to break that silence through her groundbreaking study into records of the American Freedmen's Inquiry Commission (AFIC), which reveals illicit relationships between white women and black men in the nineteenth-century South.[26]

The AFIC, "formed under the War Department of Congress, . . . [was] composed of three white anti-slavery men, [who] would ultimately propose the establishment of the Freedmen's Bureau to assist former slaves in the transition to free labor."[27] These men interviewed numerous former slaves who insisted that "it was just as common for colored men to have connection with white women, as for white men to have to do with colored women." One former slave related to the Commission his relationship with a forty-year-old widowed plantation mistress:

> The [slave], who had been "brought up in the family," said he had "never had anything to do with his mistress until after her husband died," but that almost a year into her widowhood, the woman "ordered him to sleep with her, and he did regularly."[28]

Did Mary ever engage one of her male slaves into an illicit relationship out of loneliness? Or might she have had a relationship with a white friend or in-law? The birth of a child long after her husband's death would have been proof, of course, but Mary could have known how to avoid pregnancy. Though the use of birth control to prevent unwanted pregnancies was against the customs of a Southern agrarian society that relied heavily on a large family—white and black—widows and single women wishing to avoid conception or to start a delayed menstrual period learned from newspaper advertisements and through handed-down folk remedies ways to protect themselves from unwanted pregnancies or how to terminate a pregnancy.[29] Naturally, the records about this part of her life are silent on this intimate aspect.

The outbreak of the Civil War brought new challenges. At least three of Mary's sons served in the Confederacy: John, Francis and Oscar.[30] Surprisingly, Mary's household did not suffer much during the Civil War. In 1860, her real property was valued at $7,000. After the War, in 1870, it had increased in value to $7,500. Her son John ran the plantation, which consisted of 190 acres of improved land. They owned four horses, three milch cows and fourteen swine. Their crops were winter wheat, Indian corn, oats and Irish potatoes. They also made their own butter, producing one hundred pounds of it in 1870.[31]

Having survived widowhood, running a plantation, and the Civil War, in 1881, at the age of seventy-one, Mary succumbed to death at the home of her daughter, Louisa. Mary's obituary is a testimony to her strength of character. Though she was in pain, she never cried out for relief. Her only desire was for the Lord to take her home. "In all the relations of life, as a wife, mother, friend and neighbor she endeavored to fulfill her duty, and her sweet patience and resignation under trials, the most severe loss of husband and children, reverses of fortune, and years of physical suffering endeared her to all who knew her."[32]

While Mary Fitzhugh (Stuart) Fitzhugh belonged to a minority group of women who remained widows in the antebellum South, the historical documents that record her life as a plantation mistress indicate that she met and overcame her obstacles. Details of her personal life are lost since no correspondence, diaries or account books appear to have survived for her. She is but one of many women who remain quiet in that respect. Through the research published by social historians on antebellum women, however, we are able to augment the bureaucratic records and speculate on many aspects of her life as a widowed plantation mistress.

———◆———

Every woman has a story to be told. Once you've gathered the ingredients—the genealogical sources—blend these with the relevant social history. Then take that final step to complete the recipe and write her story. Make her immortal. Because of you, she no longer needs to remain silent.

administratrix A woman assigned by the court to administer an intestate case.

concubine A woman who lives with a man to whom she is not married.

consort Companion; term for when the woman predeceased her husband.

coverture The condition or state of a married woman.

curtesy From *Black's Law Dictionary*: "The estate to which by common law a man is entitled, on the death of his wife, in the lands or tenements of which she was seised [*sic*] in possession in fee-simple or in tail during her coverture, provided they have had lawful issue born alive in which might have been capable of inheriting the estate. It is a free-hold estate for the term of his natural life."

daughtered out Genealogical term for a lineage that has no male heirs to carry on the surname.

divorce *a mensa et thoro* Divorce from bed and board. A suspension of the marital relationship in respect to cohabitation but not as to other rights and obligations, so that the parties may not marry again.

divorce *a vinculo matrimonii* Divorce from the bond of marriage; a complete dissolution of all marriage ties. A total or absolute divorce.

dower From *Black's Law Dictionary*: "The provision which the law makes for a widow out of the lands or tenements of her husband, for her support and the nurture of her children. . . . The life estate to which every married woman is entitled on death of her husband, intestate, or, in case she dissents from his will, one-third in value of all lands of which husband was beneficially seized in law or in fact, at any time during coverture."

dowry Property the bride brings to her marriage.

et al. And others.

et ux. And wife.

executrix The woman named in the will to distribute the estate.

feme covert From *Black's Law Dictionary*: "A married woman. Generally used in reference to the legal disabilities of a married woman, as compared with the condition of a *feme sole*."

feme sole From *Black's Law Dictionary*: "A single woman, including those who have been married, but whose marriage has been dissolved by death or divorce, and, for most purposes, those women who are judicially separated from their husbands."

***feme sole* trader** From *Black's Law Dictionary*: "In English law, a married woman, who, by the custom of London, trades on her own account, independently of her husband; so called because, with respect to her trading, she is the same as a *feme sole*. The term is applied also to women deserted by their husbands, who do business as *femes sole*."

grass widow A woman whose husband has deserted her; also used to refer to a woman who has illegitimate children or is a discarded common-law wife.

issue Children of a couple.

life estate An estate in land granted to one for the term of his or her life.

lying in Term used in colonial times to refer to childbirth.

mantua maker One who practices the art of fashionable dressmaking which required an apprenticeship.

matrilineal The maternal line; i.e., daughter, mother, grandmother, great-grandmother and so on.

mtDNA Mitochrondial DNA.

née Used to indicate a woman's maiden name (Sharon Carmack *née* DeBartolo).

patronymic A name derived from the name of a father or ancestor, usually by adding a suffix or prefix, such as Williamson (son of William).

primogeniture Under common law, the right of the eldest son to inherit his father's real property to the exclusion of younger sons.

relict A widow.

suffragette Term used in England to denote a woman who was for women's right to vote.

suffragist Term used in America to denote a woman who was for women's right to vote.

umbilical line The maternal line, see also *matrilineal*.

An Overview of Women's Legal Rights in America

"Married Women and the Law"

A man and wife are one person in law; the wife loses all her rights as a single woman, and her existence is entirely absorbed in that of her husband. He is civilly responsible for her acts; she lives under his protection or cover, and her condition is called coverture.

A woman's body belongs to her husband; she is in his custody, and he can enforce his right by a writ of habeas corpus.

What was her personal property before marriage, such as money in hand, money at the bank, jewels, household goods, clothes, etc., becomes absolutely her husband's, and he may assign or dispose of them at his pleasure whether he and his wife live together or not.

A wife's chattels real *(i.e., estates) become her husband's.*

Neither the Courts of Common Law nor Equity have any direct power to oblige a man to support his wife. . . .

The legal custody of children belongs to the father. During the lifetime of a sane father, the mother has no rights over her children, except a limited *power over infants, and the father may take them from her and dispose of them as he thinks fit.*

A married woman cannot sue or be sued for contracts—nor can she enter into contracts except as the agent of her husband; that is to say, her word alone is not binding in law. . . .

A wife cannot bring actions unless the husband's name is joined.

A husband and wife cannot be found guilty of conspiracy, as that offense cannot be committed unless there are two persons.

Barbara Leigh Smith Bodichon,
published in 1854, quoted in
Carolyn G. Heilbrun's,
Writing a Woman's Life

———◆———

While it is not necessary to learn in detail women's legal status throughout America's history in order to begin your genealogical research, studying the laws that pertain to women will make your research more successful. There is a tremendous variation among colonies and later, states, concerning divorce, property and inheritance laws, which continued to evolve over time, and it is certainly beyond the scope of this book to detail these laws. To become familiar with the relevant laws during a given time, see Table 7–2 in Loretto Dennis Szucs and Sandra Hargreaves Luebking's *The Source: A Guidebook of American Genealogy,* which gives a state-by-state listing of printed laws prior to 1900. These published law books are available at law libraries.

The intent in this section is to provide you with an overview to make you aware of some of the various laws and legal terms that have an impact on researching women. For example, in most colonies and later, states, it was illegal for women to vote until the Nineteenth Amendment was passed in 1920. New Jersey, however, adopted an election law in 1790 that referred to voters as "he or she." Although voting privileges for women were revoked in 1807, some of the poll lists are extant. A few of the western states passed suffrage for women as early as the mid- to late-1800s. If your female ancestor lived in New Jersey between 1790 and 1807, or in one of the western states (see the Source Checklist in Appendix C), this would affect your research since there may be extant voter lists. (See chapter two.)

The most significant legal areas affecting the search for women are divorce, property and inheritance laws (state level) and naturalization laws and widow's pension application acts (federal level).

Property, Inheritance and Divorce Laws

Laws of property and inheritance vary considerably from state to state and were constantly evolving. For example, in 1848 New York passed a law giving married women limited property rights. The act was revised in 1860, which allowed married women to not only own property, but to also keep their own wages, enter into contracts, sue and be sued in court and to have equal rights in child custody cases. Massachusetts passed a Married Women's Property Act in 1854, giving women control of their own property and the right to make wills. The Wyoming legislature approved limited married women's rights in 1869.

On some land transactions where the husband and wife are selling property, you will find an additional paragraph that states something to this effect:

> Personally appeared before the subscriber, an acting Justice of the Peace, in and for said county, Adam Losh and Ann his wife acknowledged the signing and sealing of the foregoing deed. . . . The said Ann Losh being examined separate and apart from her said husband, Adam Losh, and the contents of this deed made known to her by me, she acknowledged she executed the same freely without fear or coercion of her said husband. . . .

This is called a release of dower. Dower is different from *dowry,* which is the property (real or personal) that a wife brings into a marriage. According to *Black's Law Dictionary,* dower was "the provision which the law makes for a widow out of the lands or tenements of her husband, for her support and the nurture of her children. . . . The life estate to which every married woman is entitled on death of her husband, intestate, or, in case she dissents from his will, one-third in value of all lands of which husband was beneficially seized in law or in fact, at any time during coverture [the condition of a married woman]." In the foregoing example, Ann Losh released her dower rights so that the title of the property became free and clear. If she did not release her dower, after her husband's death, she could sue the purchaser to recover her third-interest in the property. It is not true that deeds were witnessed by someone from the wife's side of the family in order to protect her dower. A life estate meant that the land was granted to her for the term of her life. (See chapter two, Land Records.)

Some of the southern colonies established dower rights as early as the 1670s, such as Virginia and Maryland; others, such as South Carolina, did not enact a statute regarding dower until 1715. In the North, the colonies of Connecticut, Massachusetts, Pennsylvania and New York were more lax about dower acknowledgments. Connecticut did not pass any laws regarding women and property rights until 1723, Pennsylvania not until 1770 and New York didn't follow until 1771.

Donn Devine states the following in "The Widow's Dower Interest: When Its Presence or Absence is Significant," published in *Ancestry* magazine:

> You must know exactly how dower operated at a particular time and place to form a hypothesis or a con-

clusion from the presence or absence of a wife or mother's mention in a deed, will, or intestate land distribution. For example, if you found a deed from a married man which his wife had not joined in making, does it mean that she had already died or merely stayed home to take care of the children when it was made?

Under English common law used by the colonies, a married woman, also known legally as a *feme covert*, was subject to coverture. A married woman had no independent legal standing; she was "covered" by her husband. She could not own property, execute wills or enter into any kind of contract without her husband's consent. This also meant that she could not sue or be sued. Upon becoming a widow, a woman became a *feme sole*, giving her, in some jurisdictions, the right to own and sell land and to operate a business in her own name. Single and divorced women were also considered *femes sole* and had many of the same legal rights as men. (See the Glossary.)

Divorce laws and practices, which can affect child custody, alimony, property and inheritance, also varied from state to state and from one time period to another (see chapter two, Divorce Records). In a divorce of bed and board (*a mensa et thoro*), the woman remained a *feme covert*, and her husband retained control of the couple's property. As a separated *feme covert*, she was not allowed to run her own business, engage in any contracts, control property or remarry until her husband died. If an absolute divorce was granted (*a vinculo a matrimonii*), then a woman became a *feme sole*, having the right to remarry, and she might be able to regain her dowry and a portion of the couple's property.

For more information on property rights, inheritance and divorce, see Marylynn Salmon's *Women and the Law of Property in Early America*; Carole Shammas, Marylynn Salmon and Michel Dahlin's *Inheritance in America: From Colonial Times to the Present*; Linda E. Speth and Alison D. Hirsch's *Women, Family, and Community in Colonial America: Two Perspectives*; Ronald Hoffman and Peter J. Albert's *Women in the Age of the American Revolution*; and Glenda Riley's *Divorce: An American Tradition*.

Naturalization Laws

Researching immigrant women will be affected by naturalization laws, which were constantly changing as more and more newcomers arrived in this country. Prior to 1855 there were no specific references in the naturalization laws regarding women's citizenship, but between 1855 and 1922, any married woman automatically became a citizen when she married a citizen or a man who obtained citizenship. Between 1907 and 1922 a law was passed that she would retain her U.S. citizenship if the marriage ended in divorce, as long as she continued to reside in the United States or registered within one year of leaving the country. After 1922, an alien woman who married an American or someone who was naturalized did not automatically become a citizen. She had to apply on her own; however, no declaration of in-

tention was required and only one year of residency. When an American woman married a foreigner between 1907 and 1922, she lost her U.S. citizenship and took on the nationality of her husband. She would have to apply to regain her U.S. citizenship. If the marriage ended in divorce, she had to reapply for citizenship. After 1922, women did not lose their citizenship when they married non-Americans.

Widows fell into other categories of the naturalization laws. Between 1804 and 1906 a widow became a citizen if her husband had filed his declaration of intention but had died before he became naturalized. She only needed to take an oath of allegiance. After 1906, she also had to comply with the other provisions of the law, except for filing a declaration.

For more information on naturalization laws, see John J. Newman's *American Naturalization Processes and Procedures, 1790–1985*.

Widow's Pension Application Acts

The first federal act to grant pensions to widows and orphans of military officers was passed on 24 August 1780. Widows and orphans of Revolutionary War veterans were entitled to receive half of the officer's pay for seven years. Numerous other acts subsequently followed:

1832 Widows and children were entitled to receive money due to the pensioner (officers and enlisted men) if it had not been paid before he died.

1836 Widows received a pension that

would have been authorized if the veteran had still been alive. The widow had to have married the veteran either before or while he was in the service.

1838 Widows were entitled to a pension for five years if they had married a veteran prior to 1 January 1794.

1848 If a woman had married the veteran before 2 January 1800, as a widow she could receive a pension for life.

1853 The restrictions on the date a widow married the veteran were eliminated.

1864 Widows and children of black soldiers were entitled to receive pensions without proof of marriage other than that the parties had habitually recognized each other as man and wife and had lived together as such for a definite period of not less than two years to be shown by the affidavits of credible witnesses.

1866 Widows of black soldiers no longer required proof of marriage other than evidence that the parties had habitually recognized each other as

man and wife and had lived together as such.

1873 African American widows were required to supply evidence of marriage by some ceremony deemed by them obligatory.

1878 Widows were entitled to receive a lifetime pension if the veteran had served at least fourteen days or had participated in any engagement.

After the War of 1812, a widow could apply for a pension if her husband had served fourteen days or in any engagement. Widows of Mexican War veterans, if they had not remarried, were paid if the husband had served at least sixty days between 1846 and 1848. Not only widows and minor dependents, but also parents were entitled in some circumstances to receive a pension based on a veteran's service in the Civil War (Union army). Widows of Confederate soldiers had to prove financial need or physical disability to the Southern state issuing the pension. (See the Bibliography for sources pertaining to widow's pensions.)

For more information on military pensions and acts, see *Guide to Genealogical Research in the National Archives* and James C. Neagles's *U.S. Military Records: A Guide to Federal and State Sources, Colonial America to the Present.*

Matrilineal Research and Genetics

Some genealogists may be interested in researching and documenting their maternal, or umbilical, line. Instead of focusing on the paternal line, where all the males have the same surname, you follow an unbroken female line: your mother, your mother's mother, your mother's maternal grandmother and so on. The challenging part is that with each generation the surname changes and oftentimes the locality of research. It is also a fascinating aspect of genealogy if you happen to be interested in genetics.

In June 1994, an article appeared in the *National Genealogical Society Quarterly's* special issue *Your Family's Health History: An Introduction.* Written by Thomas H. Roderick, Ph.D., "Umbilical Lines and the mtDNA Project" explains:

> Each human inherits equal portions of nuclear DNA (deoxyribose nucleic acid, the "building blocks" of life) from his or her mother and father. But there are exceptions. One is the tiny but very important mitochondrial DNA (mtDNA), which lies outside the nucleus and is usually transmitted only through the umbilical line. Both males and females inherit it, but only

females pass it on. This fraction, vitally important to life, is now the subject of considerable genetic research.

So, for example, because the mtDNA would not be passed on from a male, my husband's mtDNA, which he inherited from his mother, grandmother, great-grandmother and so on, stops with him. Our daughter has inherited my mtDNA, and this is what she will pass on to her children.

Geneticists like Dr. Roderick are interested in studying the mutation rate of mtDNA over the generations. Their theory is that the mutation rate is extremely low, so that "any person should have the same mtDNA with the same umbilical ancestor as far as fifteen to twenty generations removed."

One of the most famous cases using mtDNA evidence to prove or, rather, disprove a relationship was that involving the woman who claimed to be Princess Anastasia Romanov. Her mtDNA was compared with known descendants of Anastasia's maternal line. The blood samples did not match. (For more details on this study, see Robert K. Massie's *The Romanovs: The Final Chapter* [New York: Random House, 1995].)

Another famous case was the search for the Sundance Kid in Bolivia (a Discovery Channel TV special). Collateral maternal relatives were identified, and blood or hair samples were taken to determine the mtDNA, but once again, the remains of the alleged Sundance Kid did not match the known relatives.

Another aspect of this project is that geneticists have been able to determine racial and ethnic backgrounds because the studies have also revealed different mtDNA for different groups of peoples. "So, for the genealogist," writes Dr. Roderick, "an analysis of the mtDNA of anyone living would reveal the racial and perhaps ethnic background of his or her umbilical line, information from before the time of printed records. A particularly interesting example is that of a woman from Yorkshire, [England,] who has mtDNA similar to [those] in some Middle East countries."

The mtDNA Project invites researchers who can document eight or more generations of their umbilical lines to submit their findings. The project started in 1992, and after just two years, more than three hundred pedigrees had been submitted. Most of them are of New England origin. For example, several umbilical lines have been established to *Mayflower* passenger Priscilla (Mullins) Alden. If you are interested in assisting with this project, submit your documented maternal line to the mtDNA Project, Center for Human Genetics, Municipal Building, P.O. Box 770, Bar Harbor, Maine 04609-0770.

Source Checklist for Researching Female Ancestors

Oral History

vital information (birth, marriage, death, etc.)

family traditions

everyday life as a child (school and play)

relationship with her parents, with mother in particular

onset of menstruation and young adult experiences

courtship and marriage

attitudes toward sex, birth control, family size

childbirth experience

child-raising experiences

relationship with her spouse

everyday life as a young mother and housewife

everyday life as an adult

favorite recipes

homemade artifacts (quilts, needlework, crafts, etc.)

holiday traditions

income-producing work outside the home

income from outside sources (doing laundry, ironing, sewing, selling butter and eggs, taking in boarders)

voluntary organizations or club memberships

hobbies

life accomplishments

memories of grandparents, grandmothers in particular

memories of oldest living relative during her lifetime

guiding philosophies in life

regrets

"words of wisdom" to future female generations

Home Sources

letters, postcards

diaries, journals

needlework, quilts

family Bible

birth certificates, baby books

baptism, confirmation certificates

marriage certificates, wedding albums

death records, prayer cards

funeral/memorial cards

school report cards, yearbooks, scrapbooks

recipe books

dishes, china, silverware

kitchen utensils

clothing, shoes, hats

jewelry

newspaper clippings, obituaries

photographs

postmortem photographs

deeds to houses, photographs of houses

checkbooks, bank statements

citizenship papers, passports

pension papers

wills

medical records

books, magazines

knickknacks, souvenirs

toys, games

furniture

collectibles (coins, stamps)

musical instruments

Published Sources

compiled genealogies

record abstracts, transcriptions

genealogical periodicals

local and county histories

social histories

Computer Databases at the Family History Library

International Genealogical Index (IGI)

Social Security Death Index

Ancestral File

U.S. Military Index (Korean and Vietnam wars)

Vital Records

birth

marriage

divorce, annulment

death

Church Records

baptism, christening

confirmation

membership, admission, removal

minister's journal

meeting minutes

annulment

women's group

burial

fornication confessions

Cemetery and Funeral Home Records

tombstone inscriptions

burial or interment records

mortuary, funeral home

crematorium

exhumations or grave relocations

Newspapers

Sunday women's section (starting 1860s)

local news

gossip columns

obituaries

marriage notices

anniversary celebrations

family reunions

birth announcements

unclaimed mail

legal notices

notices repudiating wives' debts

runaways (slaves, indentured servants, wives)

advice columns

major events (strikes, disasters)

classified advertisements

help wanted
ethnic newspapers

School Records

elementary
secondary
boarding schools
normal schools
ladies' seminaries
colleges and universities

Establishment of Major Women's Seminaries and Colleges

1787 Young Ladies Academy, Philadelphia

1797 Young Ladies Academy, Boston

1819 Elizabeth Female Academy/ College, Washington, Mississippi

1821 Troy Female Seminary, Troy, New York

1824 Adams Female Seminary, East Derry, New Hampshire

1827 Hartford Female Seminary, Hartford, Connecticut

1832 Western Female Institute, Cincinnati, Ohio

1833 Oberlin College, Ohio (open to all races)

1833 Columbia Female Academy (later Stephens College), Missouri

1837 Mount Holyoke Female Seminary, South Hadley, Massachusetts

1838 Georgia Female College (later Wesleyan College), Macon, Georgia

1841 Patapsco Female Institute, Maryland

1848 New England Female Medical College

1849 Rockford Female Seminary (in 1892, Rockford College), Illinois

1850 Female Medical College, Philadelphia, Pennsylvania (in 1867 became Woman's Medical College of Pennsylvania; renamed Medical College of Pennsylvania in 1970)

1851 Mary Sharp College, Tennessee

1852 Antioch College, Yellow Springs, Ohio

1855 Elmira Female College, New York

1855 University of Iowa admits women

1855 Benicia Seminary (later Mills College), California

1863 Homeopathic New York Medical College for Women

1863 University of Wisconsin accepts women

1864 Swarthmore College, near Philadelphia

1865 Vassar College, Poughkeepsie, New York

1867 Howard University, Washington, DC

1868 Women's Medical College of New York Infirmary

1868 Cornell University accepts women

1869 St. Louis Law School (later Washington University School of Law), Missouri, admits women

1869 Indiana, Kansas and Minnesota all admit women to their universities; Indiana accepts women from out of state

1870 University of Michigan, University of California, University of Illinois, University of Missouri, University of Cincinnati and Ohio State accept women

1870 Female Normal and High School (later Hunter College), New York

1870 Massachusetts Institute of Technology accepts women

1873 Evanston College for Ladies merges with Northwestern University, Illinois

1873 Boston University becomes coed

1873 Bennett Seminary (later Bennett College for Women) accepts male and female African Americans

1873 Bellevue Hospital in New York

City, Massachusetts General Hospital in Boston and Connecticut Hospital in New Haven open training schools for nurses

1875 Smith College, Massachusetts

1875 Wellesley College, Massachusetts

1875 Mount Hermon Female Seminary, Mississippi (open also to black women)

1878 Girls' Latin School, Boston, first public college prep school in Massachusetts

1879 Harvard Annex (in 1894 renamed Radcliffe College)

1881 Atlanta Baptist Seminary, for black women

1884 Women's College of Baltimore (later Goucher)

1884 Mississippi Industrial Institute and College for the Education of White Girls of the State of Mississippi

1884 Hartshorn Memorial College for Women, Richmond, Virginia

1885 Bryn Mawr College, near Philadelphia

1887 H. Sophie Newcomb Memorial College, New Orleans

1889 Barnard College, New York

1892 Brown University admits women

1892 University of Chicago admits women

1898 Washington Law School admits women, Washington, DC

1900 Trinity College, Washington, DC

1902 Simmons College for Women, Boston

1908 Portia Law School (in 1969, New England School of Law)

1918 Yale Law School admits women

1918 Marymount School, Tarrytown, New York

1918 College of William and Mary, Virginia, admits women

1919 Emmanuel College, Boston

1920 University of Virginia admits women into graduate program; undergraduate women not admitted until 1970

1950 Harvard Law School admits women

1969 Yale University admits women

1970 Princeton becomes coed

1976 Women admitted to U.S. military service academies (see references under Military, page 109)

1983 Columbia College admits women

Censuses

1790 (names head of household only)
1800   "

1810   "
1820   "
1830   "
1840   " (plus Revolutionary War pensioners and widows receiving pensions)
1850 (first to name everyone in household, birthplace and whether married within the year)
1860
1870 (whether parents foreign born)
1880 (first to name relationships to head of household)
extant 1890
1900 (number of years married, number children born and how many living, immigration and naturalization information)
1910   "
1920   "
mortality (1850, 1860, 1870, 1880)
veteran's (1890—Civil War Union veterans and widows [enumeration incomplete])
slave (1850, 1860)
Indian (special censuses)
agricultural (1850, 1860, 1870, 1880)
industry, manufacturing (extant 1820, 1850, 1860, 1870)
social statistics (1850, 1860, 1870, 1880)
1880 Schedule of Defective, Dependent, and Delinquent Classes
state and local censuses
school censuses

Land and Property Records

grants, patents
homesteads

deeds

mortgages and leases

releases of dower

surveys

warrants

tax rolls

Court Records

wills and administrations

estate inventories

guardianships

bastardy cases

fornication cases

civil cases

criminal hearings/records

divorce cases

marriage bonds, licenses, certificates

property foreclosures

brands and marks

insanity/commitment orders

adoptions

minute books

orders, judgments

coroner's files

licenses and permits

apprenticeships, indentures

name changes

military discharges

Military, Pensions, Bounty Land

colonial war service (1607–1774)

Revolutionary War and frontier conflicts
   (1775–1811)

War of 1812 (1812–15)

Indian Wars (1815–58)

Mexican War (1846–48)

Civil War (1861–65)

Spanish-American War (1898)

World War I (1917–18)

World War II (1941–45)

Korean War (1950–53)

Vietnam War (1961–73)

pension applications (for serviceperson,
   widows, mothers)

papers of the Continental Congress for
   black slaves who fled during the
   Revolution

draft records (WWI, WWII)

relocations/internment camps for
   Japanese Americans, German
   Americans and Italian Americans dur-
   ing WWII

nurses

women serving in the military

women spies, female prisoners

women serving disguised as men

Women's Voluntary, Reserve and Full-Status Military Organizations

1881 American Red Cross

1901 Army Nurse Corps (black women
      accepted in 1918)

1908 Navy Nurse Corps (only single
      women accepted until 1944; black
      women accepted as of 1945)

1917 Navy enrolls yeomanettes into
      service

1918 Marines enroll marinettes

1940 Women's Voluntary Services

1942 Women's Army Auxiliary Corps
     (WAAC); in 1943 Women's Army
     Corps (WAC)

1942 Navy's Women Accepted for Volun-
     teer Emergency Service (WAVE)

1942 Women's Auxiliary Ferrying
     Squadron and Women's Air Service
     Pilots (WASP); both merge in 1943
     as WASPs

1942 U.S. Coast Guard's SPARS

1949 Air Force Nurse Corps

Military Academies and Training Programs With Years When Women Were Accepted

1949 Air Force Officer and Candidate
     School, San Antonio, Texas

1969 Air Force Reserve Officer Training
     Corps (ROTC)

1969 Joint Armed Forces Staff College

1970 Air War College

1974 U.S. Merchant Marine Academy

1976 U.S. Naval Academy in Annapolis,
     Maryland, U.S. Military Academy in
     West Point, New York, Air Force
     Academy in Colorado Springs,
     Colorado, U.S. Coast Guard Acad-
     emy in New London, Connecticut

1995 The Citadel, Charleston, South
     Carolina

1997 Virginia Military Institute, Lexing-
     ton, Virginia

Directories

city directories
telephone directories
who's who directories
trade association directories
professional directories

Reference Guides

guides to women's studies/history
  collections
bibliographies to women's studies/
  history
bibliographies to published and manuscript diaries and correspondence
guides to dissertations

Professional Records and Organizations

midwives' registers
nurses' licenses
teachers' contracts and employment
  records
National Teachers Association founded
  1857 (1870, becomes National Education Association); admits women 1866
Association of Collegiate Alumnae, 1882;
  becomes American Association of University Women, 1921

Immigration Records

passports
passenger lists
alien registration cards
naturalization, citizenship
immigrant aid societies

Women's Organizations

local, state, regional clubs and
organizations

lineage and patriotic societies (e.g.,
Daughters of the American Revolution
and others)

sisterhoods (e.g., Rebekah Lodge, Eastern
Star, Rainbow Girls, etc.)

school sororities

Girl Scouts, Camp Fire Girls

Women's Christian Temperance Union,
founded 1874

Young Women's Christian Association,
est. 1866

National Association of Colored Women,
founded 1896

unions (e.g., International Ladies Gar-
ment Workers, Women's Trade Union
League)

state and national legislative petitions for
moral reforms (antislavery/abolition,
temperance)

Institutional Records

orphanages

almshouses, poor houses

insane asylums

hospitals

tuberculin sanatoriums

Eugenics Record Office

police records

settlement houses (e.g., Chicago's Hull
House, est. 1889)

birth control clinics (e.g., Sanger's
Planned Parenthood)

prison records (coed before establishment of women's facilities; separate
women's sections of state prisons)

Women's Prisons and Reformatories Through 1935 With Dates When Institutions Began Receiving Women Prisoners

1839 Mount Pleasant Female Prison,
New York

1873 Indiana Reformatory Institution for
Women and Girls, Indianapolis

1877 Massachusetts Reformatory Prison
for Women, Sherborn

1887 House of Refuge [for women],
Hudson, New York

1893 Western House of Refuge [for
women], Albion, New York

1901 New York State Reformatory for
Women, Bedford

1913 New Jersey State Reformatory for
Women, Clinton

1916 Maine State Reformatory for
Women, Skowhegan

1916 Ohio Reformatory for Women,
Marysville

1918 Connecticut State Farm for Women,
Niantic

1918 Iowa Women's Reformatory, Rock-
well City

1918 Kansas State Industrial Farm for
Women, Lansing

1920 Pennsylvania State Industrial Home for Women, Muncy

1920 Minnesota State Reformatory for Women, Shakopee

1920 Nebraska State Reformatory for Women, York

1920 Arkansas State Farm for Women, Jacksonville

1921 Wisconsin Industrial Home for Women, Taycheedah

1925 Rhode Island State Reformatory for Women, Cranston

1929 North Carolina Industrial Farm Colony for Women, Kinston

1930 Illinois State Reformatory for Women, Dwight

1932 Virginia State Industrial Farm for Women, Goochland

1933 California Institution for Women, Techachapi (later moved to Frontera) (Female Department of San Quentin, 1933–36)

Employment

factory
secretarial
nursing
teaching
seamstress
domestic
boardinghouse
prostitution
saloon, gambling
actress, opera house
apprenticeship
indenture
lawyer, doctor

Manuscript and Local History Collections

National Union Catalog of Manuscript Collections
letters, diaries, loose papers
Orphan Train records

Woman's Suffrage and Voter Lists and Registrations

state and national legislative petitions for woman's suffrage
woman's suffrage organizations (local, state, national)
American Woman Suffrage Association, est. 1869
National Woman Suffrage Association, est. 1869
International Woman Suffrage Alliance, est. 1902
Woman Suffrage Party of Greater New York, est. 1909
Congressional Union, est. 1913

States and years when full woman's suffrage was passed before 1920
Wyoming, 1869
Utah, 1870, abolished in 1887, reinstated in 1896
Colorado, 1893
Idaho, 1896
Washington, 1910

California, 1911

Arizona, Kansas, Oregon, 1912

Alaska, 1913

Montana, Nevada, 1914

New York, 1917

South Dakota, Oklahoma, Michigan, 1918

States with partial woman's suffrage before 1920 (e.g., women allowed to vote only in school board, local or presidential elections)

New Jersey (1776, property owners can vote, including women who meet the criteria; 1790, maids and widows, black and white, can vote; revoked 1807)

Kentucky (beginning in 1838, widowed women can vote in school board elections)

Kansas (1859, women allowed to vote in school elections; 1887 women allowed to vote in local elections)

Massachusetts (1879, women allowed to vote in school board elections)

Indiana, Michigan, Nebraska, North Dakota, Ohio and Rhode Island (1917, women allowed to vote in presidential elections)

Arkansas (1917, women may vote in the primaries)

Texas (1918, women allowed to vote in primaries)

Minnesota

Iowa

Missouri

Wisconsin

Illinois

Tennessee

Maine

Nineteenth Amendment passed, giving women nationwide the right to vote, 1920

Women's Social Histories

ethnic

time period

locality

westward expansion

published diaries

anthologies of women's letters, diaries

Prescriptive Literature for Women

Magazines

Lady's Weekly Miscellany, 1805–08

Ladies' Magazine (later *American Ladies' Magazine*), 1828–36

Lady's Book 1830–98, later *Godey's Lady's Book*, 1837

Ladies' Companion, 1834–44

Ladies' Garland, 1837–49

Ladies' Repository, 1841–76

Peterson's Ladies' Magazine, 1842–98

Home Journal, 1846–1901

Lily, 1849

Mme. Demorest's Mirror of Fashions, 1860

Lady's Magazine, 1863

Harper's Bazaar, 1867–present

Frank Leslie's Lady's Journal, 1871–81

Home Companion, 1873; in 1912 *Women's Home Companion*

Ladies' Home Journal, 1877–87

Women's Home Journal, 1878

Ladies' Home Journal, 1883–present

Good Housekeeping, 1885–present

Vogue, 1892–present

Books

cookbooks (e.g., Amelia Simmons's
American Cookery, 1796)

novels (e.g., those by E.D.E.N.
Southworth and T.S. Eliot)

advice and etiquette books (some popular examples follow)

1828 Lydia Child's *The American Frugal
Housewife*

1828 Frances Parkes's *Domestic Duties;
or Instructions to Young Married
Ladies*

1837 Lydia Sigourney's *Letters to Young
Ladies*

1839 Lydia Sigourney's *Letters to Mothers*

1841 Catharine Beecher's *A Treatise on
Domestic Economy for the Use of
Young Ladies at Home and at School*

1869 Catharine Beecher and Harriet
Beecher Stowe's *The American
Woman's Home*

1878 Eunice Beecher's *All Around the
House; or How to Make Homes
Happy*

1879 Julia Wright's *The Complete Home*

1896 Luther Emmett Holt's *The Care and
Feeding of Infants*

1909 Ellen Key's *The Century of the Child*

1912 Elizabeth Chesser's *Perfect Health
for Women and Children*

NOTES

Chapter One: Sources Created by Women

1 Family papers in the possession of Marcia Wyett, Colorado Springs, Colo.

2 Family papers in the possession of Marcia Wyett, Colorado Springs, Colo.

3 Linda Peavy and Ursula Smith, *Women in Waiting in the Westward Movement: Life on the Home Frontier* (Norman: University of Oklahoma Press, 1994), 33–34.

4 Lotte and Joseph Hamburger, *Contemplating Adultery: The Secret Life of a Victorian Woman* (New York: Fawcett Columbine, 1991), 173.

5 Mary Jane Moffat and Charlotte Painter, eds., *Revelations: Diaries of Women* (New York: Vintage Books, 1974), 14.

6 Metta L. Winter, "A Look at Quaker Diaries and Their Uses," in *A Women's Diaries: Miscellany*, ed. Jane DuPree Begos (Weston, Conn.: Magic Circle Press, 1989), 30–36.

7 Lillian Schlissel, *Women's Diaries of the Westward Journey* (New York: Schocken Books, 1982), 183.

8 Emily French's diary is located in the Special Collections at the Tutt Library, Colorado College, Colorado Springs, Colo. Her diary has been transcribed and published by Janet Lecompte as *Emily: The Diary of a Hard-Worked Woman*, by Emily French (Lincoln: University of Nebraska Press, 1987).

9 Helen Banfield Jackson's diaries are located in the Special Collections at the Tutt Library, Colorado College, Colorado Springs, Colo.

10 Lyndon H. Hart, *A Guide to Bible Records in the Archives Branch, Virginia State Library* (Richmond: Virginia State Library, 1985), 117.

11 Sara M. Evans, *Born for Liberty: A History of Women in America* (New York: The Free Press, 1989), 75, 117.

12 *Guide to the Records of the United States House of Representatives at the National Archives, 1789–1989* (Washington, DC: National Archives and Records Administration, 1989), 10 para. 1.47.

13 *Guide*, 10 para. 1.46.

14 *Guide*, 8 para. 1.30–31.

15 *Guide*, 11 para. 1.49.

Chapter 2: Sources Created About Women

1 Passenger arrival manifest listing Isabella Veneto [Vallarelli], *Canopic*, sailing from Naples, 31 Mar 1916, to Boston, 15 Apr 1916, p. 22, line 7, National Archives Microcopy T843, roll 240.

2 Sara M. Evans, *Born for Liberty: A History of Women in America* (New York: The Free Press, 1989), 159–60.

3 William Starr Easton, *Descendants of Joseph Easton, Hartford, Connecticut,*

1636–1899 (St. Paul, Minn.: n.p., 1899), 56–57.

4 East Hartford, Connecticut, Vital Records 1:54, birth of Harriet Easton, September (no date given); 1:56 death of Harriet Easton, age three weeks, September (no date given) 1849, Family History Library (FHL) Microfilm #1312794.

5 1850 Mortality Schedule, Hartford, Connecticut, Town of East Hartford, p. 46, line 16.

6 Margaret C. Klein, *Tombstone Inscriptions of King George County, Virginia* (Baltimore: Genealogical Publishing Co., 1979), 19.

7 Barbara Jean Evans, *A to Zax: A Comprehensive Dictionary for Genealogists and Historians* (Alexandria, Va.: Hearthside Press, 1995), 71.

8 1860 Mortality Schedule, Giles Co., Tennessee, Accelerated Indexing Systems Mortality Schedules Index.

9 1880 Defective, Delinquent, and Dependent Classes, Ohio, Gallia Co., Morgan Twp., p. 22, line 1.

10 1880 Defective, Delinquent, and Dependent Classes, Ohio, Gallia Co., Gallia Twp., p. 16, line 4.

11 Mary Beth Norton, *Liberty's Daughters: The Revolutionary Experience of American Women, 1750–1800* (Ithaca: Cornell University Press, 1980), 191–93.

12 Virgil D. White, *Genealogical Abstracts of Revolutionary War Pension Files* (Waynesboro, Tenn.:

National Historical Publishing Co., 1990–), 1:325.

13 Civil War pension file of James H. Goforth, #SC650–531, National Archives and Records Administration, Washington, DC.

14 Civil War pension file of Andrew Points, #219116, National Archives and Records Administration, Washington, DC.

15 Deed of sale, John Richardson to John A. Donnally et al., 20 May 1837, Gallia County, Ohio, Deeds 14:402; John Newton v. John A. Donnally, May 14, 1840, Gallia County, Ohio, Chancery Court records 1:444–47, FHL Microfilm #1303072.

16 Frederick Co., Virginia, Deeds 7:232, FHL Microfilm #0031407.

17 Wayne Co., Kentucky, Deeds 1:71.

18 Knox County, Ohio, Deeds DD:586–87, FHL Microfilm #0314051.

19 Nicholas County, Kentucky, Deeds 1:476.

20 Ruth Perkins and Judy Froggett, comps., *Minister's Certificates of Marriages Commencing the Sixth Day of Sept. Anno 1836* (Greensburg, Ky.: Green County Library, 1984), 17.

21 Madison County, Virginia, Marriages, 27 Nov 1860.

22 Eugenics Record Office, Connecticut, FHL Microfilm #1711745.

23 Northwestern Memorial Hospital Records, Chicago, Illinois. Mrs. Abram Berman, p. 81, entry 1143, FHL Microfilm #1315895; Mary Rudolph

Salaterski, [n.p. # cited], entry 56092, FHL Microfilm #1315905.

24 Jeffrey Geller and Maxine Harris, *Women of the Asylum: Voices From Behind the Walls, 1840–1945* (New York: Anchor Books, 1994), 58–68.

25 1880 federal population schedule, Ohio, Gallia Co., Harrison Twp., enumeration district 29, p. 1, dwelling 5, family 6.

26 1880 Defective, Delinquent, and Dependent Classes, Ohio, Gallia Co., Harrison Twp., p. 1, line 23.

27 Town of Greenwich, Connecticut, Probate Records and Guardianships 37:145–48, FHL Microfilm #1434416.

28 1910 federal population schedule, Connecticut, Middlesex Co., Middletown, enumeration district 306, sheet 19B.

29 Glenda Riley, *Divorce: An American Tradition* (New York: Oxford University Press, 1991).

30 Riley, *Divorce*, 36, 44.

31 Riley, *Divorce*, 62–64, 79.

32 Riley, *Divorce*, 16, 18.

33 Donald M. Schlegel, *Franklin County, Ohio, Divorces Before 1870* (Columbus, Ohio: Columbus History Service, 1983), 46–47.

34 Divorce petition of Peter Bowles, Hanover Co., Virginia, [n.p. #, loose papers], FHL Microfilm #0982030.

35 Divorce petition of Sarah Cope, Fairfield Co., Connecticut, 1773, [n.p. #, loose papers], FHL Microfilm #1673220.

36 Dade Co., Missouri, Wills 1:134–40,

FHL Microfilm #0932474.

37 *Records and Files of the Quarterly Courts of Essex County, Massachusetts*, vol. 8, 1680–1683 (Salem, Mass.: Essex Institute, 1921), 367.

38 *Records and Files of the Quarterly Courts of Essex County*, 368.

39 John D'Emilio and Estelle B. Freedman, *Intimate Matters: A History of Sexuality in America* (New York: Harper and Row, 1988), 32–34.

40 Quoted in D'Emilio and Freedman, *Intimate Matters*, 33.

41 Norton, *Liberty's Daughters*, 291.

42 Sue Heinemann, *Timelines of American Women's History* (New York: Roundtable Press, 1996), 180.

Chapter 3: Additional Sources for Ethnic Women

1 Sue Heinemann, *Timelines of American Women's History* (New York: Roundtable Press, 1996), 15, 16, 19, 22, 24.

2 Mary Beth Norton, *Liberty's Daughters: The Revolutionary Experience of American Women, 1750–1800* (Ithaca: Cornell University Press, 1980), 209–12.

3 Norton, *Liberty's Daughters*, 357, note 24.

4 Stafford Co., Virginia, Deed and Will Book 1748–63, p. 391.

5 Bucks Co., Pennsylvania, Wills 4:420, file 2055. Appreciation is due Warren Cruise of Denver, Colo., for granting

permission to quote from Derrick Kroesen's will, which will be published in an upcoming family history.

6 King George Co., Virginia, Land Causes, 1831–1833, 4 August 1831, pp. 4–10.

7 1870 population schedule, Virginia, Orange Co., p. 226.

8 Marylynn Salmon, *Women and the Law of Property in Early America* (Chapel Hill: University of North Carolina Press, 1986), 149–60.

9 Noralee Frankel, "From Slave Women to Free Women: The National Archives and Black Women's History in the Civil War Era," *Prologue* 29 (summer 1997): 100–101.

10 Frankel, "From Slave Women to Free Women," 102.

11 Sara M. Evans, *Born for Liberty: A History of Women in America* (New York: The Free Press, 1989), 152, 156.

12 Quoted in Doris Weatherford's *Foreign and Female: Immigrant Women in America, 1840–1930* (New York: Schocken Books, 1986), 49.

Chapter 4: Methods for Determining Maiden Names and Parents

1 George H.S. King, "Maiden Names Used After Marriage," *The American Genealogist* 47 (1971): 44.

2 Patricia Law Hatcher, "Mary Hale, Wife of Deacon Edward Putnam, Accuser in the Salem Witchcraft Trials," *The American Genealogist* 69 (October 1994): 212–18.

3 Elizabeth Shown Mills, "Finding Females: Wives, Mothers, Daughters, Sisters, and Paramours!" (Rochester, N.Y.: lecture presented at the Federation of Genealogical Societies Conference, 1996).

4 Sandra Hargreaves Luebking, "Finding Females on the Frontier: Records and Strategies Using Nineteenth-Century Midwest Examples" (Nashville: lecture presented at the National Genealogical Society Conference, 1996).

5 1880 federal population schedule, Ohio, Gallia Co., Harrison Twp., enumeration district 29, p. 1, dwelling 5, family 6.

6 1900 federal population schedule, Ohio, Gallia Co., Harrison Twp., enumeration district 34, sheet 3, dwelling 45, family 45 (Nancy is enumerated in the household of her daughter and son-in-law, Mary and John H. Price). 1900 federal population schedule, Ohio, Gallia Co., Green Twp., enumeration district 31, sheet 3, dwelling 49, family 50 (Henry is enumerated with his son, William H.). 1870 federal population schedule, Ohio, Gallia Co., Harrison Twp., p. 1, dwelling 1, family 1; 1860 federal population schedule, Ohio, Gallia Co., Harrison Twp., p. 386, dwelling 513, family 513; 1850 federal population schedule, Ohio, Gallia Co., Perry Twp., p. 49, dwelling 1964, family 1954.

7 Gallia Co., Ohio, Probate Court, Marriage Records 1:339, Family

History Library (FHL) Microfilm #0317652.

8 Gallia Co., Ohio, Probate Records, Will of Andrew Donnally, 1:113; Will of Katherine Donnally, 1:369; Will of Peter Donnally, 1:239.

9 Henrietta C. Evans and Mary P. Wood, *Abstracts of Gallia County Chancery Records, 1835–52* (privately published, 1984), 64; original document, Gallia Co., Ohio, Chancery Court 3:504–09, FHL Microfilm #1303073.

10 Evans and Wood, *Abstracts of Gallia County Chancery Records*, 16; original document, Gallia Co., Ohio, Chancery Court 1:444–47, FHL Microfilm #1303072.

11 Evans and Wood, *Abstracts of Gallia County Chancery Records*, 67; original document, Gallia Co., Ohio, Chancery Court 3:582–85, FHL Microfilm #1303073.

12 Evans and Wood, *Abstracts of Gallia County Chancery Records*, 11; original document, Gallia Co., Ohio, Chancery Court 1:208–13, FHL Microfilm #1303072.

13 Gallia Co., Ohio, Deeds 27:52, FHL Microfilm #0317687.

14 Gallia Co. Ohio, Grantor Index, 1789–1892, FHL Microfilm #0317673; Gallia Co., Ohio, Grantee Index, 1789–1892, FHL Microfilm #0317674.

15 *Cemeteries of Harrison Township, Gallia County, Ohio* (Gallipolis, Ohio: Gallia County Historical Society, 1980), 15.

16 Gallia Co., Ohio, Probate Court, Record of Deaths, p. 46, #221, FHL Microfilm #0317663.

17 1840 federal population schedule, Ohio, Gallia Co., Green Twp., p.59.

18 Birth years are calculated from the 1850 federal population schedule, Kentucky, Green Co., p. 101, dwelling 311, family, 310; 1860 federal population schedule, Kentucky, Green Co., p. 605, dwelling 466, family 462; 1870 federal population schedule, Kentucky, Green Co., p. 32, dwelling 213, family 226.

19 Ruth Perkins and Judy Froggett, comps., *Minister's Certificates of Marriages Commencing the Sixth Day of Sept. Anno 1836* (Greensburg, Ky.: Green County Library, 1984), 17.

20 Barbara Wright, *Green County, Kentucky, Will Records, Book III, 1840–1875* (privately published, n.d.).

21 Green County, Kentucky, Wills, 1793–1913, FHL Microfilms #0594634–35.

22 1850 federal population schedule, Kentucky, Green Co., p. 115, dwelling 506, family 506, district 1.

23 1830 federal population schedule, Kentucky, Green Co., p. 4.

Chapter 5: Writing About Women Ancestors

1 Ann Jones, *Women Who Kill* (New York: Fawcett Columbine, 1980), 28; James Kendall Hosmer, *Winthrop's Journal: "History of New England" 1630–1649* (New York: Barnes and

Noble, 1908) 1:282.

2 Laurel Thatcher Ulrich, *Good Wives: Image and Reality in the Lives of Women in Northern New England, 1650–1750* (New York: Oxford University Press, 1983), 196–201.

3 Barbara Mayer Wertheimer, *We Were There: The Story of Working Women in America* (New York: Pantheon Books, 1977), 248.

4 Sara M. Evans, *Born for Liberty: A History of Women in America* (New York: The Free Press, 1989), 132–134.

5 Records for the Pullman Company may be obtained by writing to the South Suburban Genealogical and Historical Society, P.O. Box 96, South Holland, Illinois, 60473.

6 David T. Courtwright, *Dark Paradise: Opiate Addiction in America Before 1940* (Cambridge: Harvard University Press, 1982), 41.

7 C. Vann Woodward, ed., *Mary Chesnut's Civil War* (New Haven: Yale University Press, 1981).

8 Evans, *Born for Liberty*, 150.

9 All information about Cicely (Penny) Chapin, her husband and her children came from Howard Millar Chapin, *Life of Deacon Samuel Chapin, of Springfield* (Providence: Snow and Farnham Co., 1908), 41–47; Gilbert Warren Chapin, *The Chapin Book of Genealogical Data* (Hartford, Conn.: Chapin Family Association, 1924), 1:vii, viii, ix, xi–xiii; and Howard Millar Chapin, "The English Ancestry of Dea. Samuel Chapin of Springfield, Mass.," *New England Historical and Genealogical Register* 83 (July 1929): 352–54.

10 Chapin, *Life of Deacon Samuel Chapin*, 41–47.

11 Chapin, *Life of Deacon Samuel Chapin*, 41–47.

12 David Hackett Fischer, *Albion's Seed: Four British Folkways in America* (New York: Oxford University Press, 1989), 140; George Francis Dow, *Every Day Life in the Massachusetts Bay Colony* (New York: Dover Publications, 1988), 62; Alice Morse Earle, *Customs and Fashions in Old New England* (New York: Charles Scribner's Sons, 1893), 320.

13 Chapin, *Life of Deacon Samuel Chapin*, 41.

14 Fischer, *Albion's Seed*, 136–37; Ulrich, *Good Wives*, 19–20.

15 Chapin, "The English Ancestry," 252–54.

16 Orange County, Virginia, Deed Book 39:258–60.

17 Orange County, Virginia, Deed Book 39:258–60.

18 Orange County, Virginia, Deed Book 39:258–60; Evans, *Born For Liberty*, 108–10; Jacqueline Jones, *Labor of Love, Labor of Sorrow: Black Women, Work, and the Family From Slavery to the Present* (New York: Basic Books, 1985), 13–43.

19 All information about the Banoni family has come from censuses: 1900 federal population schedule,

New York, Manhattan, enumeration district 126; 1905 New York state census, Manhattan, election district 12, assembly district 6; 1910 federal population schedule, Manhattan, enumeration district 116; 1915 New York state census, New York City, election district 13, assembly district 1; 1925 New York state census, New York City, election district 29, assembly district 2. Specific page numbers have been omitted to respect privacy.

20 1900 federal population schedule, New York, Manhattan, enumeration district 126; 1910 federal population schedule, Manhattan, enumeration district 116; 1915 New York state census, New York City, election district 13, assembly district 1.

21 Richard Gambino, *Blood of My Blood: The Dilemma of the Italian-Americans* (Garden City, N.Y.: Anchor Press, 1974), 178–80; Phyllis H. Williams, *South Italian Folkways in Europe and America: A Handbook for Social Workers, Visiting Nurses, School Teachers, and Physicians* (New Haven: Yale University Press, 1938), 106; Elizabeth Ewen, *Immigrant Women in the Land of Dollars: Life and Culture on the Lower East Side, 1890–1925* (New York: Monthly Review Press, 1985), 130–33; Doris Weatherford, *Foreign and Female: Immigrant Women in America, 1840–1930* (New York: Schocken Books, 1986), 2–14.

Chapter 6: A Case Study of Mary Fitzhugh (Stuart) Fitzhugh

1 Mary's birth is calculated from the 1850 federal population census, Orange Co., Va., p. 260, line 7; 1860 federal population census, Orange Co., Va., p. 71, line 16; 1870 federal population census, Orange Co., Va., p. 226, line 35.

2 King George Co., Virginia, Marriages, 1786–1850, p. 32, Family History Library (FHL) Microfilm #0032053.

3 The Fitzhugh family has been covered in many historical and genealogical publications on Virginia. Following is only a partial suggestion for more information: Richard Beale Davis, ed., *William Fitzhugh and His Chesapeake World, 1676–1701: The Fitzhugh Letters and Other Documents* (Chapel Hill: University of North Carolina Press, 1963); Jon Kukla, *Speakers and Clerks of the Virginia House of Burgesses, 1643–1776* (Richmond: Virginia State Library, 1981); *Genealogies of Virginia Families From the Virginia Magazine of History and Biography*, vol. 2 (Baltimore: Genealogical Publishing Co., 1981); Marie Fitzhugh, *Three Centuries Passed: The Fitzhugh Family* (San Antonio, Texas: The Naylor Co., 1975).

4 For information on the Stuart family, see Stella Pickett Hardy, *Colonial Families of the Southern States of America* (Baltimore: Genealogical

Publishing Co., 1968), 492–98.

5   Birth years on the Fitzhugh children, except Battaile, are calculated from the 1850 federal population census, Orange Co., Va., p. 260. The Fitzhugh children's births, including Battaile's, are also given in *Genealogies of Virginia Families*, 2:864.

6   Will of James Madison Fitzhugh, dated 8 May 1844, recorded 24 March 1845, Will Book 10:263–64, Orange Co., Va.

7   Five years before James Madison Fitzhugh's death, he owned fourteen slaves, as reported in the 1840 federal population schedule, Greene Co., Va., p. 427. Five years after his death, Mary Fitzhugh reported owning ten slaves on the 1850 slave schedule, Orange Co., Va., p. 805, line 34.

8   Henry and Sarah (Battaile) Fitzhugh of King George Co., Va., were Mary and James's great-grandparents. See note 3 for references to the Fitzhugh genealogy.

9   Catherine Clinton, *The Plantation Mistress: Woman's World in the Old South* (New York: Pantheon Books, 1982), 37–38, 44, 59, 61.

10 This term was used by slaveholders in their correspondence, diaries and conversations. See Eugene Genovese's " 'Our Family, White and Black': Family and Household in the Southern Slaveholders' World View," in *In Joy and In Sorrow: Women, Family, and Marriage in the Victorian South, 1830–1900*, ed. Carol Bleser (New York: Oxford University Press, 1991).

11 Clinton, *The Plantation Mistress*, 18–29; quote from p. 28.

12 Clinton, *The Plantation Mistress*, 47–50; Elizabeth Fox-Genovese, *Within the Plantation Household: Black and White Women of the Old South* (Chapel Hill: University of North Carolina Press, 1988), 137.

13 Fox-Genovese, *Within the Plantation Household*, 110.

14 1840 federal population schedule, Green Co., Va., p. 427.

15 Fox-Genovese, *Within the Plantation Household*, 86; Clinton, *The Plantation Mistress*, 184.

16 Clinton, *The Plantation Mistress*, 73, 201; John D'Emilio and Estelle B. Freedman, *Intimate Matters: A History of Sexuality in America* (New York: Harper and Row, 1988), 94. See also Catherine Clinton, "Southern Dishonor: Flesh, Blood, Race, and Bondage," in *In Joy and In Sorrow*, ed. Bleser.

17 1850 slave schedule, Orange Co., Va., p. 805, line 34.

18 Deed of Trust between James M. Fitzhugh, James B. Newman and Mary F. Fitzhugh, dated 29 January 1844, Orange Co., Va., Deed Book 39:258–60.

19 Will of James Madison Fitzhugh.

20 Carole Shammas, Marylynn Salmon, and Michel Dahlin, *Inheritance in America: From Colonial Times to the Present* (New Brunswick: Rutgers

University Press, 1987), 67–72; Fox-Genovese, *Within the Plantation Household*, 203, 206; Clinton, *The Plantation Mistress*, 78.

21 1850 federal population census, Orange Co., Va., p. 260, line 7; 1860 federal population census, Orange Co., Va., p. 71, line 16; 1870 federal population census, Orange Co., Va., p. 226.

22 1860 federal population schedule, Orange Co., Va., p. 71, line 6. For further study on the relationship between plantation mistress and overseer, see Joan Cashin, "Since the War Broke Out: The Marriage of Kate and William McLure," in *Divided Houses: Gender and the Civil War*, ed. Catherine Clinton and Nina Silber, (New York: Oxford University Press, 1992), 200–12.

23 Clinton, *The Plantation Mistress*, 102, 164–65; 1850 federal population schedule, Orange Co., Va., p. 260, line 7.

24 Clinton, *The Plantation Mistress*, 170–71; David T. Courtwright, *Dark Paradise: Opiate Addiction in America Before 1940* (Cambridge: Harvard University Press, 1982), 36–43, 56–61.

25 Clinton, *The Plantation Mistress*, 199–211; quote from D'Emilio and Freedman, *Intimate Matters*, 104.

26 Martha Hodes, "Wartime Dialogues on Illicit Sex: White Women and Black Men," in *Divided Houses*, ed. Clinton and Silber.

27 Hodes, "Wartime Dialogues," 232.

28 Hodes, "Wartime Dialogues," 235.

29 Hodes, "Wartime Dialogues," 236. Also see Sharon DeBartolo Carmack's "Immigrant Women and Family Planning: Historical Perspectives for Genealogical Research," *National Genealogical Society Quarterly* 84, no. 2 (June 1996): 102–14.

30 Confederate States of America, Virginia, index: John Stuart Fitzhugh, Family History Library (FHL) Microfilm #0029786 and #0881413; Francis Conway Fitzhugh, FHL #0029786; Oscar Stuart Fitzhugh, FHL #0029786 and #0881413.

31 1870 Orange Co., Va., agricultural schedule, page 23, line 6, John S. Fitzhugh.

32 Obituary for Mary Fitzhugh (Stuart) Fitzhugh, typed transcript from the *Washington Star* (no place, date or page number cited) sent to the compiler by Mary Eleanor Fitzhugh Hitselberger, Fon du Lac, Wisconsin.

BIBLIOGRAPHY

Please note: This is by no means a comprehensive listing of all materials that will help in your search on female ancestors. Many more books and articles are available on women's subjects.

Genealogical Case Studies and Articles Involving Research on Women

Anderson, Robert Charles. "Abigail, Wife of Samuel Gay (1663–1753) of Roxbury and Swansea, Massachusetts, and Lebanon, Connecticut." *The Genealogist* 1 (1980): 72–79.

Bjorkman, Gwen Boyer. "Hannah (Baskel) Phelps Phelps Hill: A Quaker Woman and Her Offspring." *National Genealogical Society Quarterly* 75 (December 1987): 289–302.

Blanton, DeAnne. "Women Soldiers of the Civil War." *Prologue: The Quarterly of the National Archives* 25, no. 1 (Spring 1993): 27–33.

Carmack, Sharon DeBartolo. "Immigrant Women and Family Planning: Historical Perspectives for Genealogical Research." *National Genealogical Society Quarterly* 84, no. 2 (June 1996): 102–14.

———. "Learning About Jewish Immigrant Women: Fact and Fiction." *Avotaynu: The International Review of Jewish Genealogy* 12, no. 3 (Fall 1996): 24–26.

Cerny, Johni, and Arlene Eakle. "Tracing the Women in Your Family." In *Ancestry's Guide to Research: Case Studies in American Genealogy.* Salt Lake City: Ancestry Publishing, 1985.

Devine, Donn. "The Widow's Dower Interest: When Its Presence or Absence is Significant." *Ancestry* (September-October 1994): 20–22.

Eakle, Arlene H. "How to Trace Your Pedigree Ladies." Unpublished paper at the Family History Library in Salt Lake City, Utah, 1988.

Frankel, Noralee. "From Slave Women to Free Women: The National Archives and Black Women's History in the Civil War Era." *Prologue: The Quarterly of the National Archives* 29, no. 2 (summer 1997): 100–104.

Hatcher, Patricia Law. "Mary Hale, Wife of Deacon Edward Putnam, Accuser in the Salem Witchcraft Trials." *The American Genealogist* 69, no. 4 (October 1994): 212–18.

———. "A Multiplicity of Marys: Corrections and Additions to Genealogies of the Abbott, Hale, Hovey, Jackson, and Jewett Families of Essex County, Massachusetts." *The American Genealogist* 68, no. 2 (April 1993): 77–83.

Hogan, Roseann R. "Female Ancestry." *Ancestry* (March-April 1994): 26–28.

Joslyn, Roger D. "Abigail (Wells) (Wetmore) Seward of Durham, Connecticut: Wife of

Jabez Wetmore and Ephraim Seward." *The American Genealogist* 72, no. 2 (April 1997): 81–88.

King, George H.S. "Maiden Names Used After Marriage." *The American Genealogist* 47 (1971): 44.

Lenzen, Connie. "Proving a Maternal Line: The Case of Frances B. Whitney." *National Genealogical Society Quarterly* 82, no. 1 (March 1994): 17–31.

Mills, Elizabeth Shown. "The Search for Margaret Ball: Building Steps Over a Brick-Wall Research Problem." *National Genealogical Society Quarterly* 77 (March 1989): 43–65.

Mills, Elizabeth Shown, and Sharon Scholars Brown. "In Search of 'Mr. Ball': An Exercise in Finding Fathers." *National Genealogical Society Quarterly* 80, no. 2 (June 1992): 115–33.

Peters, Bette D. "Colorado's 'Mother Cawker' and Her Offspring." *National Genealogical Society Quarterly* 78, no. 2 (June 1990): 115–34.

Randall, Katharine P. "Those Early Firstborns of Eighteenth-Century America: Moral Lapses or Planned Parenthood?" *The New York Genealogical and Biographical Record* 115 (April 1984): 78–87.

Remington, Gordon L. "James Jewett of Jeremysquam: A *Maine Families in 1790* Case Study." *The Maine Genealogist* 19, no. 1 (February 1997): 3–16.

Richardson, Douglas. "Evidence for Four Generations of a Matrilineal Line." *The New England Historical and Genealogical Register* 148, no. 591 (July 1994): 240–54.

Rising, Marsha Hoffman. "Researching Women in Land Conveyances: Groton, Connecticut, Deeds, Volume 5, 1743–1760." *The American Genealogist* 69, no. 1 (January 1994): 15–21.

———. "The Search for Mary Ann Spangler: Narrowing a Field of Potential Parents." *National Genealogical Society Quarterly* 77 (September 1989): 197–207.

Wakefield, Robert S. "The 'Only Girl in Town' Theory: The Case of Mary Cooke, Wife of Caleb Johnson of Haddam, Connecticut." *The American Genealogist* 72, no. 1 (January 1997): 39–41.

Conference Lectures on Audiocassette Tape
Order from Repeat Performance, 2911 Crabapple Lane, Hobart, Indiana 46342; (219) 465-1234.

Bamman, Gale Williams. "But I Just Don't Love You Anymore! Divorce in Antebellum America." S-139. Rochester, N.Y.: Federation of Genealogical Societies Conference, 1996.

Carmack, Sharon DeBartolo. "The Silent Woman: Bringing a Name to Life." NE-59. Boston, Mass: New England Historic Geneaological Society Sesquicentennial Conference, 1995.

Holcomb, Brent. "Women in South Carolina Records: When, Where, Why?" VA-89.

Richmond: Federation of Genealogical Societies Conference, 1994.

Leary, Helen F.M. "The Better Half: North Carolina Women's Genealogy." VA-50. Richmond: Federation of Genealogical Societies Conference, 1994.

Luebking, Sandra Hargreaves. "Finding Females on the Frontier: Records and Strategies Using Nineteenth-Century Midwest Examples." W-19. Nashville: National Genealogical Society Conference, 1996.

Melchiori, Marie Varrelman. "But Grandma Never Carried a Gun: Locating Women Using Records Created by the Military." S-125. Rochester, N.Y.: Federation of Genealogical Societies Conference, 1996.

Mills, Elizabeth Shown. "Finding Females: Wives, Daughters, Mothers, Sisters, and Paramours!" T-25. Rochester, N.Y.: Federation of Genealogical Societies Conference, 1996.

Potter, Constance. "Liberty's Daughters: Finding Women in the Revolution." T-63. Valley Forge: National Genealogical Society Conference, 1997.

Schoeffler, William. "And the Widow Gets Her Thirds: Dower Rights and Other Clues to Women in Property Records." BM-151-A. Baltimore: National Genealogical Society Conference, 1993.

Wylie, Barbara Brixey. "Was Your Grandmother a Relict? What Do Those Old Words Mean?" W-25. Valley Forge: National Genealogical Society Conference, 1997.

Genealogical Research Guides and Articles

American Indians: A Select Catalog of National Archives Microfilm Publications. Washington, D.C.: National Archives Trust Fund Board, 1984.

Bell, Mary McCampbell, Clifford Dwyer, and William Abbott Henderson. "Finding Manuscript Collections: NUCMC, NIDS, and RLIN." *National Genealogical Society Quarterly* 77, no. 3 (September 1989): 208–18.

Berry, Ellen Thomas, and David Allen Berry. *Our Quaker Ancestors: Finding Them in Quaker Records.* Baltimore: Genealogical Publishing Co., 1987. Reprint, 1996.

Black, Henry Campbell. *Black's Law Dictionary.* 6th ed. St. Paul: West Publishing Co., 1990.

Black Studies: A Select Catalog of National Archives Microfilm Publications. Washington, D.C.: National Archives Trust Fund Board, 1984.

Byers, Paula K., ed. *Native American Genealogical Sourcebook.* New York: Gale Research, 1995.

Carmack, Sharon DeBartolo. *The Genealogy Sourcebook.* Los Angeles: Lowell House, 1997.

Crandall, Ralph. *Shaking Your Family Tree.* Dublin, N.H.: Yankee Publishing Co., 1986.

Croom, Emily Anne. *Unpuzzling Your Past: A Basic Guide to Genealogy.* 3rd ed. Cincinnati: Betterway Books, 1995.

Doane, Gilbert H., and James B. Bell. *Searching for Your Ancestors: The How and Why of Genealogy*. 6th ed. Minneapolis: The University of Minnesota Press, 1992.

Eichholz, Alice, ed. *Ancestry's Red Book: American State, County, and Town Sources*. Rev. ed. Salt Lake City: Ancestry Publishing, 1989.

Epstein, Ellen, and Jane Lewit. *Record and Remember: Tracing Your Roots Through Oral History*. Lanham, Md.: Scarborough House, 1994.

Evans, Barbara Jean. *A to Zax: A Comprehensive Dictionary for Genealogists and Historians*. 3rd ed. Alexandria, Va.: Hearthside Press, 1995.

Everton, George B., comp. *The Handy Book for Genealogists*. 8th ed. Logan, Utah: Everton Publishers, 1991.

Greenwood, Val D. *The Researcher's Guide to American Genealogy*. 2nd ed. Baltimore: Genealogical Publishing Co., 1990.

Guide to Genealogical Research in the National Archives. Washington, DC: National Archives Trust Fund Board, 1985.

Guide to the Records of the United States House of Representatives at the National Archives, 1789–1989. Washington, DC: National Archives and Records Administration, 1989.

Guide to the Records of the United States Senate at the National Archives, 1789–1989. Washington, DC: National Archives and Records Administration, 1989.

Hatten, Ruth Land. "The 'Forgotten' Census of 1880: Defective, Dependent, and Delinquent Classes." *National Genealogical Society Quarterly* 80 (March 1992): 57–70.

Hill, Edward E. *Guide to Records in the National Archives of the United States Relating to American Indians*. Washington, DC: National Archives and Records Service, 1981.

Hone, E. Wade. *Land and Property Research in the United States*. Salt Lake City: Ancestry Publishing, 1997.

Luebking, Sandra Hargreaves, and Loretto Dennis Szucs. *Family History Made Easy: A Step-by-Step Guide to Discovering Your Heritage*. Salt Lake City: Ancestry Publishing, 1998.

Mokotoff, Gary. *How to Document Victims and Locate Survivors of the Holocaust*. Teaneck, N.J.: Avotaynu, 1995.

Newman, John J. *American Naturalization Processes and Procedures, 1790–1985*. Indianapolis: Indiana Historical Society, 1985.

Periodical Source Index (PERSI) [to genealogical articles and case studies]. Fort Wayne, Ind.: Allen County Public Library Foundation, annual since 1986.

Rising, Marsha Hoffman. "Accumulating Negative Evidence." *Association of Professional Genealogists Quarterly* 4, no. 3 (fall 1989): 66–68.

Roderick, Thomas H. "Umbilical Lines and the mtDNA Project." *National Genealogical*

Society Quarterly 82, no. 2 (June 1994): 144–45.

————— et al. "Files of the Eugenics Record Office: A Resource for Genealogists." *National Genealogical Society Quarterly* 82, no. 2 (June 1994): 97–113.

Rose, Christine. *Nicknames: Past and Present.* 2nd ed. San Jose, Calif.: Rose Family Association, 1995.

Rubincam, Milton. *Pitfalls in Genealogical Research.* Salt Lake City: Ancestry Publishing, 1987.

Ryskamp, George R. "Fundamental Common-Law Concepts for the Genealogist: Marriage, Divorce, and Coverture." *National Genealogical Society Quarterly* 83, no. 3 (September 1995): 165–79.

Schaefer, Christina K. *Guide to Naturalization Records of the United States.* Baltimore: Genealogical Publishing Co., 1997.

Streets, David H. *Slave Genealogy: A Research Guide With Case Studies.* Bowie, Md.: Heritage Books, 1986.

Stryker-Rodda, Harriet. *How to Climb Your Family Tree.* Baltimore: Genealogical Publishing Co., 1977. Reprint, 1987.

Szucs, Loretto Dennis, and Sandra Hargreaves Luebking. *The Archives: A Guide to the National Archives Field Branches.* Salt Lake City: Ancestry Publishing, 1988.

—————. *The Source: A Guidebook of American Genealogy.* Rev. ed. Salt Lake City: Ancestry Publishing, 1997.

Thackery, David T., and Dee Woodtor. *Case Studies in Afro-American Genealogy.* Chicago: The Newberry Library, 1989.

Walton-Raji, Angela. *Black Indian Genealogy Research: African American Ancestors Among the Five Civilized Tribes.* Bowie, Md.: Heritage Books, 1993.

Wines, Frederick Howard. *Report on the Defective, Dependent, and Delinquent Classes of the Population of the United States.* Washington, DC: Government Printing Office, 1888.

Witcher, Curt B. *A Bibliography of Sources for Native American Family History.* Fort Wayne, Ind.: Allen County Public Library, 1988.

—————. "Jewish and Eastern European Treasures: Right at Your Fingertips." *Ancestry* 15 (June-July 1997): 42–46.

Sampling of Abstracted Records Relating to Women

Bamman, Gale W., and Debbie W. Spero. *Tennessee Divorces, 1797–1858, Taken From 750 Legislative Petitions and Acts.* Thorndike, Mass.: Van Volumes Ltd., 1990.

Gorin, Michelle Bartley. *South Central Kentucky Vital Statistics: Births and Deaths for Slaves and Black Families.* Glasgow, Ky.: Gorin Genealogical, 1994.

Hawbaker, Gary T. *Runaways, Rascals, and Rogues: Missing Spouses, Servants and*

Slaves: Abstracts from Lancaster County, Pennsylvania, Newspapers. Hershey, Penn.: privately published, 1987.

Headley, Robert K. *Genealogical Abstracts From the 18th Century Virginia Newspapers.* Baltimore: Genealogical Publishing Co., 1987.

Meier, Judith Ann. *Runaway Women: Elopements and Other Miscreant Deeds of Women, as Advertised in the Pennsylvania Gazette.* Apollo, Penn.: Closson Press, 1993.

Sanborn, Melinde Lutz. *Lost Babes: Fornication Abstracts From Court Records, Essex County, Massachusetts, 1692–1745.* Derry, N.H.: privately published, 1992.

Smith, Billy G., and Richard Wojtowicz, comps. *Blacks Who Stole Themselves: Advertisements for Runaways in the Pennsylvania Gazette, 1728–1790.* Philadelphia: University of Pennsylvania, 1989.

Stampp, Kenneth, ed. *Records of Ante-Bellum Southern Plantations From the Revolution through the Civil War.* Frederick, Md.: University Publications of America, 1985. Microfilm.

Tregillis, Helen Cox. *River Roads to Freedom: Fugitive Slave Notices and Sheriff Notices Found in Illinois Sources.* Bowie, Md.: Heritage Publishers, 1988.

Windley, Lathan A. *Runaway Slave Advertisements: A Documentary History From the 1730s to 1790.* 4 vols. Westport, Conn.: Greenwood Press, 1983.

Microfilms Relating to Military Pensions in the National Archives, Record Group 15: Records of the Veterans Administration

Revolutionary War

M804: Revolutionary War Pension and Bounty-Land Warrant Application Files

Civil War (Union)

T288: General Index to Pension Files, 1861–1934

T289: Organization Index to Pension Files of Veterans Who Served Between 1861 and 1900 (Army nurses on rolls 746–47)

War of 1812

M313: Index to the War of 1812 Pension Application Files

Mexican War

T317: Index to Mexican War Pension Files, 1887–1926

Indian War

T318: Index to Indian War Pension Files, 1892–1929

Remarried Widows Index (filed under current woman's name, then will reference the veteran)

M1784: Index to Pension Application Files of Remarried Widows Based on Service in the War of 1812, Indian War, Mexican War, and Regular Army Before 1861.

M1785: Index to Pension Application Files of Remarried Widows Based on Service in the Civil War and Later Wars and in the Regular Army After the Civil War.

Published Finding Aids and Indexes to Pension Files

Beers, Henry Putney. *The Confederacy: A Guide to the Archives of the Government of the Confederacy States of America.*

Washington, DC: National Archives and Records Administration, 1986.

Bockstruck, Lloyd DeWitt. *Revolutionary War Bounty Land Grants Awarded by State Governments*. Baltimore: Genealogical Publishing Co., 1996.

A Census of Pensioners for Revolutionary or Military Services. Washington, DC: Department of State, 1841. Reprint, Baltimore: Genealogical Publishing Co., 1967.

Index of Revolutionary War Pension Applications in the National Archives. National Geneaological Society Special Publication, no. 40. Washington, DC: National Genealogical Society, 1976.

Military Service Records: A Select Catalog of National Archives Microfilm Publications. Washington, DC: National Archives Trust Fund Board, 1985.

Neagles, James C. *U.S. Military Records: A Guide to Federal and State Sources, Colonial America to the Present*. Salt Lake City: Ancestry Publishing, 1994.

White, Virgil D. *Genealogical Abstracts of Revolutionary War Pension Files*. 4 vols. Waynesboro, Tenn.: National Historical Publishing Co., 1990–.

————. *Index to War of 1812 Pension Files*. 3 vols. Waynesboro, Tenn.: National Historical Publishing Co., 1989.

Legislative Petitions in the National Archives

The following list was extracted from *Guide to the Records of the United States House of Representatives at the National Archives,* *1789–1989* (cited on page 126), p. 213, para. 14.52, 14.72, 14.73; p. 299, para. 22.56; and *Guide to the Records of the United States Senate at the National Archives, 1789–1989* (see page 126), p. 149, para. 13.32; p. 154, para. 13.63. Note: The first numbers after "HR" or "SEN" (House of Representatives or Senate) indicate the session of Congress. The years of that Congress are in brackets for your convenience and are not part of the original citation. There may be other records (dockets, minute books, committee papers, etc.) among the files that also include petitions and memorials. The listings below are not all-inclusive; there are more petitions found in other House and Senate committees, as well. (See chapter 1 for information on accessing these records.)

Abolition of Slavery—Petitions and Memorials: Records of the U.S. House of Representatives (Record Group 233), Records of the Judiciary Committee, Committee on the Judiciary.

> HR 27A-G10.7 [1841–43]
> HR 28A-G10.2 [1843–45]
> HR 30A-G9.2 [1847–49]
> HR 32A-G10.3 [1851–53]
> HR 36A-G10.5 [1859–61]
> HR 37A-G7.1 [1861–63]
> HR 37A-G7.2 [1861–63]
> HR 38A-G10.1 [1863–65]

Woman Suffrage—Petitions and Memorials: Records of the U.S. Senate (Record Group 46), Records of the Committee on the

Judiciary, 1861–1901 (37th–56th Congresses), Committee on the Judiciary.

SEN 40A-H10.3 [1867–69]
SEN 41A-H10 [1869–71]
SEN 41A-H10.1 [1869–71]
SEN 42A-H11.4 [1871–73]
SEN 43A-H11.1 [1873–75]
SEN 43A-H11.3 [1873–75]
SEN 46A-H11.1 [1879–81]
SEN 46A-H11.2 [1879–81]
SEN 54A-J19.3 [1895–97]
SEN 56A-J21.2 [1899–1901]

Woman Suffrage—Petitions and Memorials: Records of the U.S. Senate (Record Group 46), Records of the Committee on the Judiciary, Records of the Select and Standing Committees on Woman Suffrage (1881–1921).

SEN 63A-J85 [1913–15]
SEN 63A-K15 [1913–15]
SEN 64A-K9 [1915–17]
SEN 65A-J56 [1917–19]
SEN 65A-K11 [1917–19]

Alcohol Temperance—Petitions and Memorials: Records of the U.S. House of Representatives (Record Group 233), Records of the Select Committees of the House of Representatives, Select Committee on Alcoholic Liquor Traffic (1879–1893).

HR 46A-H25.1–3 [1879–81]
HR 47A-F31.1–2 [1881–83]
HR 47A-H23.1 [1881–83]
HR 48A-F37.1–2 [1883–85]
HR 48A-H31.1–2 [1883–85]

HR 50A-H31.1 [1887–89]
HR 51A-F43.1–3 [1889–91]
HR 51A-H24.1–7 [1889–91]
HR 52A-F46.1–2 [1891–93]
HR 52A-H25.1–3 [1891–93]

Women's and General Social History Sources

Albers, Patricia, and Beatrice Medicine, eds. *The Hidden Half: Studies of Plains Indian Women.* Washington, DC: University Press of America, 1983.

America: History and Life (A Guide to Periodical Literature). Santa Barbara: ABC-Clio, Inc., annual.

Anthony, Susan B., et al. *The History of Woman Suffrage.* 4 vols. Indianapolis: Hollenbeck Press, 1902.

Arksey, Laura, Nancy Pries, and Marcia Reed. *American Diaries: An Annotated Bibliography of Published American Diaries and Journals.* Detroit: Gale Research Co., 1983, 1987.

Bailey, Beth L. *From Front Porch to Backseat: Courtship in Twentieth-Century America.* Baltimore: Johns Hopkins University Press, 1988.

Barker-Benfield, G.J., and Catherine Clinton, eds. *Portraits of American Women from Settlement to the Present.* New York: St. Martin's Press, 1991.

Bataille, Gretchen M., ed. *Native American Women: A Biographical Dictionary.* New York: Garland, 1993.

Bataille, Gretchen M., and Kathleen Mullen Sands. *American Indian Women: Telling*

Their Lives. Lincoln: University of Nebraska Press, 1984.

Baum, Charlotte, Paula Hyman, and Sonya Michel. *The Jewish Woman in America*. New York: Dial Press, 1976.

Begos, Jane DuPree, ed. *A Women's Diaries: Miscellany*. Weston, Conn.: Magic Circle Press, 1989.

Berlin, Ira. *Slaves Without Masters: The Free Negro in the Antebellum South*. New York: Pantheon Books, 1974.

Berlin, Ira, and Ronald Hoffman, eds. *Slavery and Freedom in the Age of the American Revolution*. Charlottesville: University Press of Virginia, 1983.

Blair, Karen J. *The History of American Women's Voluntary Organizations, 1810–1960: A Guide to Sources*. Boston: G.K. Hall and Co., 1989.

Blake, Nelson Manfred. *The Road to Reno: A History of Divorce in the United States*. New York: Macmillan, 1962.

Bleser, Carol, ed. *In Joy and In Sorrow: Women, Family, and Marriage in the Victorian South, 1830–1900*. New York: Oxford University Press, 1991.

Blumenthal, Walter Hart. *Brides From Bridewell: Female Felons Sent to Colonial America*. Westport, Conn.: Greenwood Press, 1962.

Bordin, Ruth. *Woman and Temperance: The Quest for Power and Liberty, 1873–1900*. Philadelphia: Temple University Press, 1981.

Borer, Mary Irene Cathcart. *Willingly to School: A History of Women's Education*. Guilford and London: Lutterworth Press, 1975.

Brackman, Barbara. *Clues in the Calico: A Guide to Identifying and Dating Antique Quilts*. McLean, Va.: EPM Publications, 1989.

Brinton, Howard Haines. *Quaker Journals: Varieties of Religious Experience Among Friends*. Wallingford, Pa.: Pendle Hill Publications, 1972.

Brockett, L.P., and Mary C. Vaughan. *Women at War: A Record of Their Patriotic Contributions, Heroism, Toils, and Sacrifice During the Civil War*. 1867. Reprint, Woodbury, N.Y.: Longmeadow, 1993.

Brodie, Janet Farrell. *Contraception and Abortion in Nineteenth-Century America*. Ithaca: Cornell University Press, 1994.

Buhle, Mari Jo, and Paul Buhle, eds. *The Concise History of Woman Suffrage: Selections from the Classic Work of Stanton, Anthony, Gage, and Harper*. Urbana: University of Illinois Press, 1978.

Bullough, Vern L., and Bonnie Bullough. *Women and Prostitution: A Social History*. Buffalo: Prometheus Books, 1987.

Butler, Anne M. *Daughters of Joy, Sisters of Misery: Prostitutes in the American West, 1865–1890*. Urbana: University of Illinois Press, 1985.

Campbell, D'Ann. "Women's Life in Utopia: The Shaker Experience in Sexual Equality

Reappraised: 1810 to 1860." *New England Quarterly* 51 (March 1978): 23–38.

Child, Lydia Maria. *The American Frugal Housewife*. 1828. Reprint, Cambridge: Applewood Books.

Claghorn, Charles E. *Women Patriots of the American Revolution: A Biographical Dictionary*. Metuchen, N.J.: Scarecrow Press, 1991.

Clinton, Catherine. *The Other Civil War: American Women in the Nineteenth Century*. New York: Hill and Wang, 1984.

———. *The Plantation Mistress: Woman's World in the Old South*. New York: Pantheon Books, 1982.

———. *Tara Revisited: Women, War, and the Plantation Legend*. New York: Abbeville Press, 1995.

Clinton, Catherine, and Nina Silber, eds. *Divided Houses: Gender and the Civil War*. New York: Oxford University Press, 1992.

Cohen, Miriam. *Workshop to Office: Two Generations of Italian Women in New York City, 1900–1950*. Ithaca: Cornell University Press, 1992.

Colman, Penny. *Spies! Women in the Civil War*. Cincinnati: Betterway Books, 1992.

Constructing a Revolution: Women and Gender Roles in Virginia. Thematic Issue. *The Virginia Magazine of History and Biography* 104, no. 2 (spring 1996).

Conway, Jill K. *The Female Experience in Eighteenth- and Nineteenth-Century America: A Guide to the History of American Women*. New York: Garland, 1982. Reprint, Princeton: Princeton University Press, 1985.

———. "Perspectives on the History of Women's Education in the United States." *History of Education Quarterly* 15 (1974).

Cott, Nancy F. *The Bonds of Womanhood: "Woman's Sphere" in New England, 1780–1835*. New Haven: Yale University Press, 1977.

Courtwright, David T. *Dark Paradise: Opiate Addiction in America Before 1940*. Cambridge: Harvard University Press, 1982.

Cowan, Ruth Schwartz. *More Work for Mother: The Ironies of Household Technology From the Open Hearth to the Microwave*. New York: Basic Books, 1983.

Craik, Elizabeth, ed. *Marriage and Property: Women and Marital Customs in History*. Aberdeen: Aberdeen University Press, 1991.

Croly, Jane C. *The History of the Woman's Club Movement in America*. New York: H.G. Allen, 1898. Microfilm.

Cullen-DuPont, Kathryn. *The Encyclopedia of Women's History in America*. New York: Facts on File, 1996.

Culley, Margo, ed. *A Day at a Time: The Diary Literature of American Women from 1764 to the Present*. New York: The Feminist Press at the City University of New York, 1985.

Daniels, Roger. *Coming to America: A History of Immigration and Ethnicity in*

American Life. New York: HarperCollins, 1990.

Danky, James P., ed. *Women's Periodicals and Newspapers from the Eighteenth Century to 1981.* Boston: G.K. Hall and Co., 1982.

Dannet, Sylvia G.L., ed. *Noble Women of the North.* New York: Thomas Yoseloff, 1959.

Davies, Margery W. *Woman's Place Is at the Typewriter: Office Work and Office Workers, 1870–1930.* Philadelphia: Temple University Press, 1982.

Davison, Jane, and Lesley Davison. *To Make a House a Home: Four Generations of American Women and the Houses They Lived In.* New York: Random House, 1994.

Degler, Carl N. *At Odds: Women and the Family in America From the Revolution to the Present.* New York: Oxford University Press, 1980.

D'Emilio, John, and Estelle B. Freedman. *Intimate Matters: A History of Sexuality in America.* New York: Harper and Row, 1988.

De Pauw, Linda Grant. *Founding Mothers: Women in America in the Revolutionary Era.* Boston: Houghton Mifflin, 1975.

De Pauw, Linda Grant, and Conover Hunt. *"Remember the Ladies": Women in America, 1750–1815.* New York: The Viking Press, 1976.

Dexter, Elisabeth Anthony. *Colonial Women of Affairs: Women in Business and the Professions in America Before 1776.* 2nd ed. Boston: Houghton Mifflin, 1931.

Dick, Everett. *The Dixie Frontier: A Social History.* New York: Knopf, 1948.

Diner, Hasia R. *Erin's Daughters in America: Irish Immigrant Women in the Nineteenth Century.* Baltimore: Johns Hopkins University Press, 1983.

Donegan, Jane B. *Women and Men Midwives: Medicine, Morality and Misogyny in Early America.* Westport, Conn.: Greenwood Press, 1978.

Douglas, Susan J. *Where the Girls Are: Growing Up Female With the Mass Media.* New York: Times Books, 1994.

Dow, George Francis. *Every Day Life in the Massachusetts Bay Colony.* New York: Dover Publications, 1988.

Dublin, Thomas. *Transforming Women's Work: New England Lives in the Industrial Revolution.* Ithaca: Cornell University Press, 1994.

Dunn, Mary Maples. "Saints and Sisters: Congregational and Quaker Women in the Early Colonial Period," *American Quarterly* 30 (winter 1978): 582–601.

Earle, Alice Morse. *Customs and Fashions in Old New England.* New York: Charles Scribner's Sons, 1893.

———. *Home Life in Colonial Days.* 1898. Reprint, Stockbridge, Mass.: Berkshire House, 1992.

East, Charles, ed. *Sarah Morgan: The Civil War Diary of a Southern Woman.* New York: Simon and Schuster, 1992.

Edmonds, Mary Jaene. *Samplers and Samplermakers: An American Schoolgirl Art, 1700—1850*. New York: Rizzoli International Publications, 1991.

Ehrenreich, Barbara, and Deirdre English. *For Her Own Good: 150 Years of the Experts' Advice to Women*. New York: Anchor Press, 1978.

Evans, Sara M. *Born for Liberty: A History of Women in America*. New York: The Free Press, 1989.

Ewen, Elizabeth. *Immigrant Women in the Land of Dollars: Life and Culture on the Lower East Side, 1890–1925*. New York: Monthly Review Press, 1985.

Fairbanks, Carol, and Sara Brooks Sundberg. *Farm Women on the Prairie Frontier: A Sourcebook for Canada and the United States*. Metuchen, N.J.: The Scarecrow Press, 1983.

Farr, Sidney Saylor. *Appalachian Women: An Annotated Bibliography*. Lexington: University Press of Kentucky, 1981.

Faust, Drew Gilpin. *Mothers of Invention: Women of the Slaveholding South in the American Civil War*. Chapel Hill: University of North Carolina Press, 1996.

Finkelstein, Barbara J. "Schooling and Schoolteachers: Selected Bibliography of Autobiographies in the Nineteenth Century." *History of Education Quarterly* 14 (1974): 293–300.

Fischer, David Hackett. *Albion's Seed: Four British Folkways in America*. New York: Oxford University Press, 1989.

Fischer, Gayle V., comp. *Journal of Women's History: Guide to Periodical Literature*. Bloomington: Indiana University Press, 1992.

Fisher, Helen E. *Anatomy of Love: The Natural History of Monogamy, Adultery, and Divorce*. New York: W.W. Norton and Co., 1992.

Flower, Margaret. *Victorian Jewellery*. South Brunswick, N.J.: A.S. Barnes and Co., 1967.

Forbes, Harriette, comp. *New England Diaries, 1602–1800: A Descriptive Catalogue of Diaries, Orderly Books and Sea Journals*. Published privately, 1923. Reprint, New York: Russell and Russell, 1967.

Formanek-Brunell, Miriam. *Made to Play House: Dolls and the Commercialization of American Girlhood, 1830–1930*. New Haven: Yale University Press, 1993.

Fox-Genovese, Elizabeth. *Within the Plantation Household: Black and White Women of the Old South*. Chapel Hill: University of North Carolina Press, 1988.

Franklin, Penelope, ed. *Private Pages: Diaries of American Women, 1830s–1970s*. New York: Ballantine Books, 1986.

Freedman, Estelle B. *Their Sisters' Keepers: Women's Prison Reform in America, 1830–1930*. Ann Arbor: University of Michigan Press, 1981.

Friedman, Jean E. *The Enclosed Garden: Women and Community in the Evangelical*

South, 1830–1900. Chapel Hill: University of North Carolina Press, 1985.

Gabaccia, Donna. *From the Other Side: Women, Gender, and Immigrant Life in the U.S., 1820–1990.* Bloomington: Indiana University Press, 1994.

Geller, Jeffrey, and Maxine Harris. *Women of the Asylum: Voices From Behind the Walls, 1840–1945.* New York: Anchor Books, 1994.

Gilbert, Victor Francis, and Darshan Singh Tatla, comps. *Women's Studies: A Bibliography of Dissertations, 1870–1982.* New York: Basil Blackwell, 1985.

Gluck, Sherna Berger, ed. *From Parlor to Prison: Five American Suffragists Talk About Their Lives.* New York: Vintage Books, 1976.

———. *Rosie the Riveter Revisited: Women, the War, and Social Change.* New York: New American Library, 1987.

Goodfriend, Joyce D., comp. *The Published Diaries and Letters of American Women: An Annotated Bibliography.* Boston: G.K. Hall and Co., 1987.

Gordon, Julia Weber. *My Country School Diary: An Adventure in Creative Teaching.* New York: Dell Publishing, 1946.

Gordon, Linda. *Woman's Body, Woman's Right: A Social History of Birth Control in America.* New York: Penguin Books, 1977.

Green, Harvey. *The Light of the Home: An Intimate View of the Lives of Women in Victorian America.* New York: Pantheon Books, 1983.

———. *The Uncertainty of Everyday Life, 1915–1945.* New York: HarperCollins, 1992.

Green, Rayna. *Native American Women: A Contextual Bibliography.* Bloomington: Indiana University Press, 1983.

———. *Women in American Indian Society.* New York: Chelsea House, 1992.

Greenwald, Maurine Weiner. *Women, War, and Work: The Impact of World War I on Women Workers in the United States.* Westport, Conn.: Greenwood Press, 1980.

Grossberg, Michael. *Governing the Hearth: Law and the Family in Nineteenth-Century America.* Chapel Hill: University of North Carolina Press, 1985.

Guillet, Edwin C. *The Great Migration: The Atlantic Crossing by Sailing-Ship Since 1770.* Toronto: University of Toronto, 1963.

Gutman, Herbert. *The Black Family in Slavery and Freedom, 1750–1925.* New York: Vintage Books, 1976.

Hagood, Margaret Jarman. *Mothers of the South: Portraiture of the White Tenant Farm Woman.* Chapel Hill: University of North Carolina Press, 1939.

Hale, Judson, ed. *The Best of the Old Farmer's Almanac: The First 200 Years.* New York: Random House, 1991.

Hall, Richard. *Patriots in Disguise: Women*

Warriors of the Civil War. New York: Paragon House, 1993.

Hampsten, Elizabeth. *Read This Only to Yourself: The Private Writings of Midwestern Women, 1880–1910.* Bloomington: Indiana University Press, 1982.

Harrison, Cynthia Ellen, ed. *Women in American History: A Bibliography.* 2 vols. Santa Barbara: ABC-Clio Books, 1979.

Hartog, Hendrik. "Lawyering, Husbands' Rights, and the 'Unwritten' Law in Nineteenth-Century America." *The Journal of American History* 84, no. 1 (June 1997): 67–96.

Harvey, Brett. *The Fifties: A Women's Oral History.* New York: HarperCollins, 1993.

Hawke, David Freeman. *Everyday Life in Early America.* New York: Harper and Row, 1988.

Heinemann, Sue. *Timelines of American Women's History.* New York: Roundtable Press, 1996.

Hinding, Andrea, ed. *Women's History Sources: A Guide to Archives and Manuscript Collections in the United States.* 2 vols. New York: R.R. Bowker, 1979.

Hine, Darlene Clark, et al., eds. *Black Women in America: An Historical Encyclopedia.* 2 vols. Bloomington: Indiana University Press, 1994.

Hoffer, Peter C., and N.E.H. Hull. *Murdering Mothers: Infanticide in England and New England, 1558–1803.* New York: New York University Press, 1981.

Hoffert, Sylvia D. *Private Matters: American Attitudes Toward Childbearing and Infant Nurture in the Urban North, 1800–1860.* Urbana: University of Illinois Press, 1989.

Hoffman, Ronald, and Peter J. Albert, eds. *Women in the Age of the American Revolution.* Charlottesville: The University Press of Virginia, 1989.

Holmes, Kenneth L., ed. *Covered Wagon Women: Diaries and Letters From the Western Trails, 1840–1890.* 11 vols. Spokane: The Arthur H. Clark Co., various years.

Hull, N.E.H. *Female Felons: Women and Serious Crime in Colonial Massachusetts.* Urbana: University of Illinois Press, 1987.

Humphreys, Nancy K. *American Women's Magazines: An Annotated Historical Guide.* New York: Garland, 1989.

Hurmence, Belinda, ed. *Before Freedom: Forty-eight Oral Histories of Former North and South Carolina Slaves.* New York: Mentor Press, 1990.

Hymowitz, Carol, and Michaele Weissman. *A History of Women in America.* New York: Bantam Books, 1978.

Index to Personal Names in the National Union Catalog of Manuscript Collections, 1959–1984. Alexandria, Va.: Chadwyck-Healey, 1988.

Ireland, Norma O. *Index to Women of the World From Ancient to Modern Times.* Westwood, Mass.: F.W. Faxon Co., 1970.

Jacobs, Philip P. *The Campaign Against Tuberculosis in the United States, Including a Directory of Institutions Dealing With Tuberculosis in the United States and Canada.* New York: Charities Publication Committee, 1908.

Jensen, Joan M. *Loosening the Bonds: Mid-Atlantic Farm Women, 1750–1850.* New Haven: Yale University Press, 1986.

Jones, Ann. *Women Who Kill.* New York: Holt, Rinehart, and Winston, 1980.

Jones, Jacqueline. *Labor of Love, Labor of Sorrow: Black Women, Work, and the Family From Slavery to the Present.* New York: Basic Books, 1985.

Jones-Eddy, Julie. *Homesteading Women: An Oral History of Colorado, 1890–1950.* New York: Twayne Publishers, 1992.

Jordan, Teresa. *Cowgirls: Women of the American West.* New York: Anchor Press, 1982.

Juster, Norton, comp. *A Woman's Place: Yesterday's Women in Rural America.* Golden, Colo.: Fulcrum Publishings, 1996.

Kandall, Stephen R. *Substance and Shadow: Women and Addiction in the United States.* Cambridge: Harvard University Press, 1996.

Karlsen, Carol F. *The Devil in the Shape of a Woman: Witchcraft in Colonial New England.* New York: Norton Publishers, 1987.

Katzman, David M. *Seven Days a Week: Women and Domestic Service in Industrializing America.* New York: Oxford University Press, 1978.

Kaufman, Polly Welts. *Women Teachers on the Frontier.* New Haven: Yale University Press, 1984.

Koehler, Lyle. *A Search for Power: The "Weaker Sex" in Seventeenth-Century New England.* Urbana: University of Illinois Press, 1980.

Kolodny, Annette. *The Land Before Her: Fantasy and Experience of the American Frontiers, 1630–1860.* Chapel Hill: University of North Carolina Press, 1984.

Krause, Corinne Azen. *Grandmothers, Mothers, and Daughters: Oral Histories of Three Generations of Ethnic American Women.* Boston: Twayne Publishers, 1991.

Kulikoff, Allan. "The Origins of Afro-American Society in Tidewater Maryland and Virginia, 1700 to 1790." *William and Mary Quarterly* 3rd ser. XXXV (1978): 226–59.

Larkin, Jack. *The Reshaping of Everyday Life, 1790–1840.* New York: Harper and Row, 1988.

Leavitt, Judith Walzer. *Brought to Bed: Childbearing in America, 1750–1950.* New York: Oxford University Press, 1986.

———, ed. *Women and Health in America: Historical Readings.* Madison: University of Wisconsin Press, 1984.

Lebsock, Suzanne. *Virginia Women, 1600–1945: "A Share of Honour."* Richmond: Virginia State Library, 1987.

Lieblich, Julia. *Sisters: Lives of Devotion and Defiance*. New York: Ballantine Books, 1992.

Litoff, Judy B. *American Midwives, 1860 to the Present*. Westport, Conn.: Greenwood Press, 1978.

Lerner, Gerda. *Black Women in White America: A Documentary History*. New York: Vintage, 1973.

———. *The Female Experience: An American Documentary*. Indianapolis: Bobbs-Merrill, 1977.

———. *The Majority Finds its Past: Placing Women in History*. New York: Oxford University Press, 1979.

———. *The Woman in American History*. Menlo Park, Calif.: Addison-Wesley, 1971.

Levy, JoAnn. *They Saw the Elephant: Women in the California Gold Rush*. Norman: University of Oklahoma Press, 1992.

Loeb, Catherine R., Susan E. Searing, and Esther F. Stineman. *Women's Studies: A Recommended Core Bibliography, 1980–1985*. Littleton, Colo.: Libraries Unlimited, 1987.

Lorie, Peter. *Superstitions*. New York: Simon and Schuster, 1992.

Lunardini, Christine. *What Every American Should Know About Women's History*. Holbrook, Mass.: Adams Media Corporation, 1997.

Lystra, Karen. *Searching the Heart: Women, Men, and Romantic Love in Nineteenth-Century America*. New York: Oxford University Press, 1989.

MacDonald, Anne L. *No Idle Hands: The Social History of American Knitting*. New York: Ballantine Books, 1988.

Marcus, Jacob Rader. *The American Jewish Woman, 1654–1980*. New York: Ktav Publishing House, 1981.

Marsh, Margaret, and Wanda Ronner. *The Empty Cradle: Infertility in America From Colonial Times to the Present*. Baltimore: Johns Hopkins University Press, 1996.

Mattes, Merrill J. *Platte River Road Narratives*. Urbana: University of Illinois Press, 1988.

Matthews, Glenna. *"Just a Housewife": The Rise and Fall of Domesticity in America*. New York: Oxford University Press, 1987.

Matthews, William, comp. *American Diaries: An Annotated Bibliography of American Diaries Written Prior to the Year 1861*. Berkeley: University of California Press, 1945.

———. *American Diaries in Manuscript, 1580–1954: A Descriptive Bibliography*. Athens: The University of Georgia Press, 1974.

May, Elaine Tyler. *Great Expectations: Marriage and Divorce in Post-Victorian America*. Chicago: University of Chicago Press, 1980.

McCausland, Robert R., and Cynthia

MacAlman McCausland, eds. *The Diary of Martha Ballard, 1785–1812*. Camden, Maine: Picton Press, 1992.

Melosh, Barbara. *"The Physician's Hand": Work Culture and Conflict in American Nursing*. Philadelphia: Temple University Press, 1982.

Metzker, Isaac, ed. *A Bintel Brief: Sixty Years of Letters From the Lower East Side to the Jewish Daily Forward*. Garden City, N.Y.: Doubleday and Co., 1971.

Mintz, Steven, and Susan Kellogg. *Domestic Revolutions: A Social History of American Family Life*. New York: The Free Press, 1988.

Mohr, James C. *Abortion in America: The Origins and Evolution of National Policy, 1800–1900*. New York: Oxford University Press, 1978.

Myres, Sandra L. *Westering Women and the Frontier Experience, 1800–1915*. Albuquerque: University of New Mexico Press, 1982.

Namias, June. *White Captives: Gender and Ethnicity on the American Frontier*. Chapel Hill: University of North Carolina Press, 1993.

National Union Catalog of Manuscript Collections. Washington, DC: Library of Congress, annual since 1959.

Niethammer, Carolyn. *Daughters of the Earth: The Lives and Legends of American Indian Women*. New York: Collier Books, 1977.

Norton, Mary Beth. "Eighteenth-Century American Women in Peace and War: The Case of the Loyalists." *William and Mary Quarterly* 3rd ser. XXXIII (1976), 386–98.

———. "The Fate of Some Black Loyalists of the American Revolution." *Journal of Negro History* LVIII (1973): 402–26.

———. *Liberty's Daughters: The Revolutionary Experience of American Women, 1750–1800*. Boston: Little, Brown, 1980.

O'Meara, Walter. *Daughters of the Country: The Women of the Fur Traders and Mountain Men*. New York: Harcourt, Brace and World, 1968.

Osterud, Nancy Grey. *Bonds of Community: The Lives of Farm Women in Nineteenth-Century New York*. Ithaca: Cornell University Press, 1991.

Pease, Jane H., and William H. Pease. *Ladies, Women and Wenches: Choice and Constraint in Antebellum Charleston and Boston*. Chapel Hill: University of North Carolina Press, 1990.

Peavy, Linda, and Ursula Smith. *Women in Waiting in the Westward Movement: Life on the Home Frontier*. Norman: University of Oklahoma Press, 1994.

Peiss, Kathy. *Cheap Amusements: Working Women and Leisure in Turn-of-the-Century New York*. Philadelphia: Temple University Press, 1986.

Perdue, Charles L. Jr., Thomas E. Barden, and Robert K. Phillips, eds. *Weevils in the*

Wheat: Interviews with Virginia Ex-Slaves. Charlottesville: University of Virginia Press, 1976.

Philbrook, Mary. "Woman's Suffrage in New Jersey Prior to 1807." *Proceedings of the New Jersey Historical Society*, LVII (1939): 870–98.

Pole, J.R. "Suffrage in New Jersey, 1790–1807." *Proceedings of the New Jersey Historical Society*, LXXI (1953): 39–61.

Poulos, Paula Nassen, ed. *A Woman's War Too: U.S. Women in the Military in World War II*. Washington, DC: National Archives Trust Fund Board, 1996.

Purdy, Virginia C., and Robert Gruber. *American Women and the U.S. Armed Forces: A Guide to the Records of Military Agencies in the National Archives Relating to American Women*. Originally compiled by Charlotte Palmer Seeley. Rev. ed. Washington, DC: National Archives Trust Fund Board, 1992.

Quarles, Benjamin. *The Negro in the American Revolution*. Chapel Hill: University of North Carolina Press, 1961.

———. *The Negro in the Civil War*. New York: Russell and Russell, 1968.

Rafter, Nicole Hahn. *Partial Justice: Women in State Prisons, 1800–1935*. Boston: Northeastern University Press, 1985.

Riley, Glenda. *Building and Breaking Families in the American West*. Albuquerque: University of New Mexico Press, 1996.

———. *Divorce: An American Tradition.* New York: Oxford University Press, 1991.

———. *The Female Frontier: A Comparative View of Women on the Prairie and the Plains*. Lawrence: University Press of Kansas, 1988.

———. *Women and Indians on the Frontier, 1825–1915*. Albuquerque: University of New Mexico Press, 1984.

Rothman, Ellen K. *Hands and Hearts: A History of Courtship in America*. New York: Basic Books, 1984.

Rothman, Sheila M. *Living in the Shadow of Death: Tuberculosis and the Social Experience of Illness in American History*. New York: Basic Books, 1994.

———. *Woman's Proper Place: A History of Changing Ideals and Practices, 1870 to the Present*. New York: Basic Books, 1978.

Ruether, Rosemary Radford, and Rosemary Skinner Keller, eds. *Women and Religion in America*. 3 vols. San Francisco: Harper and Row, 1981–86.

Rutman, Darrett B., and Anita H. Rutman. "Now-wives and Sons-in-law: Parental Death in a Seventeenth Century Virginia County." In *The Chesapeake in the Seventeenth Century: Essays on Anglo-American Society.*, ed. Thad W. Tate and David L. Ammerman. Chapel Hill: University of North Carolina Press, 1979.

Ryan, Mary P. *Womanhood in America: From Colonial Times to the Present*. New York: New Viewpoints/Franklin Watts, 1984.

Salmon, Marylynn. *Women and the Law of Property in Early America*. Chapel Hill: University of North Carolina Press, 1986.

Schlereth, Thomas J. *Victorian America: Transformations in Everyday Life, 1876–1915*. New York: HarperCollins, 1991.

Schlissel, Lillian. *Women's Diaries of the Westward Journey*. New York: Schocken Books, 1982.

———, et al. *Far From Home: Families of the Westward Journey*. New York: Schocken Books, 1989.

Schneider, Dorothy, and Carl J. Schneider. *American Women in the Progressive Era, 1900–1920*. New York: Anchor Books, 1994.

Scholten, Catherine M. *Childbearing in American Society: 1650–1850*. New York: New York University Press, 1985.

Shammas, Carole, Marylynn Salmon, and Michel Dahlin. *Inheritance in America: From Colonial Times to the Present*. 1987. Reprint, Galveston, Tex.: Frontier Press, 1997.

Sherr, Lynn, and Jurate Kazickas. *Susan B. Anthony Slept Here: A Guide to American Women's Landmarks*. New York: Times Books, 1994.

Shinn, Henry. "An Early New Jersey Poll List." *Pennsylvania Magazine of History and Biography*. XLIV (1920): 77–81.

Shukert, Elfrieda Berthiaume, and Barbara Smith Scibetta. *War Brides of World War II*. New York: Penguin Books, 1989.

Simmons, Amelia. *The First American Cookbook: A Facsimile of "American Cookery," 1796*. Reprint, New York: Dover Publications, 1984.

Six Women's Slave Narratives. New York: Oxford University Press, 1988.

Smith, Daniel Blake. *Inside the Great House: Planter Family Life in Eighteenth-Century Chesapeake Society*. Ithaca: Cornell University Press, 1980.

Solomon, Barbara Miller. *In the Company of Educated Women: A History of Women and Higher Education in America*. New Haven: Yale University Press, 1985.

Speth, Linda E., and Alison D. Hirsch. *Women, Family, and Community in Colonial America: Two Perspectives*. New York: Haworth Press, 1983.

Spruill, Julia Cherry. *Women's Life and Work in the Southern Colonies*. Chapel Hill: University of North Carolina Press, 1938. Reprint, New York: Norton, 1972.

Stage, Sarah. *Female Complaints: Lydia Pinkham and the Business of Women's Medicine*. New York: W.W. Norton, 1979.

Stansell, Christine. *City of Women: Sex and Class in New York, 1789–1860*. Urbana: University of Illinois Press, 1986.

Sterling, Dorothy. *Black Foremothers: Three Lives*. Old Westbury, N.Y.: Feminist Press, 1979.

———, ed. *We Are Your Sisters: Black Women in the Nineteenth Century*. New York: W.W. Norton, 1984.

Strasser, Susan. *Never Done: A History of American Housework*. New York: Pantheon Books, 1982.

Stratton, Joanna L. *Pioneer Women: Voices From the Kansas Frontier*. New York: Simon and Schuster, 1981.

Sturtz, Linda L. "The Ladies and the Lottery: Elite Women's Gambling in Eighteenth-Century Virginia." *The Virginia Magazine of History and Biography* 104, no. 2 (spring 1996): 165–84.

Sutherland, Daniel E. *The Expansion of Everyday Life, 1860–1876*. New York: Harper and Row, 1989.

Swan, Susan Burrows. *Plain and Fancy: American Women and Their Needlework, 1700–1850*. New York: Holt, Rinehart, and Winston, 1977.

Thompson, Catherine E. *A Selective Guide to Women-Related Records in the North Carolina State Archives*. Raleigh: North Carolina State Archives, 1977.

Tucker, Cynthia Grant. *Prophetic Sisterhood: Liberal Women Ministers of the Frontier, 1880–1930*. Bloomington: Indiana University Press, 1994.

Turner, Edward Raymond. "Women's Suffrage in New Jersey." *Smith College Studies in History* I, no. 4 (Northampton, 1916): 165–87.

Ulrich, Laurel Thatcher. *Good Wives: Image and Reality in the Lives of Women in Northern New England, 1650–1750*. New York: Oxford University Press, 1983.

———. "Of Pens and Needles: Sources in Early American Women's History." *The Journal of American History* 77 (June 1990): 200–207.

Weatherford, Doris. *American Women's History*. New York: Prentice-Hall, 1994.

———. *Foreign and Female: Immigrant Women in America, 1840–1930*. New York: Schocken Books, 1986.

Weinberg, Sydney Stahl. *The World of Our Mothers: The Lives of Jewish Immigrant Women*. New York: Schocken Books, 1988.

Weiner, Lynn. *From Working Girl to Working Mother: The Female Labor Force in the United States, 1820–1980*. Chapel Hill: University of North Carolina Press, 1985.

Weisberg, D. Kelley, ed. *Women and the Law: The Social Historical Perspective*. 2 vols. Cambridge: Schenkman Publishing Co., 1982.

Wells, Mildred White. *Unity in Diversity: The History of the General Federation of Women's Clubs*. Washington, DC: General Federation of Women's Clubs, 1953.

Wertheimer, Barbara Mayer. *We Were There: The Story of Working Women in America*. New York: Pantheon Books, 1977.

Wertz, Richard W., and Dorothy C. Wertz. *Lying-In: A History of Childbirth in America*. New Haven: Yale University Press, 1989.

Westin, Jeane. *Making Do: How Women Survived the '30s*. Chicago: Follett Publishing, 1976.

White, Deborah Gray. *Ar'n't I a Woman: Female Slaves in the Plantation South.* New York: W.W. Norton, 1985.

Wiley, Bell Irvin. *Confederate Women.* New York: Barnes and Noble Books, 1994.

Willard, Frances Elizabeth. *Woman and Temperance: Or, the Work and Workers of the Woman's Christian Temperance Union.* 1897. Reprint, New York: Arno Press, 1972.

Woloch, Nancy. *Women and the American Experience.* New York: Knopf, 1984.

Woody, Thomas. *A History of Women's Education in the United States.* New York: The Science Press, 1929.

Wright, Luella Margaret. *Literary Life of the Early Friends, 1650–1725.* New York: Columbia University Press, 1932.

Zophy, Angela Howard, ed. *Handbook of American Women's History.* New York: Garland Press, 1990.

Examples of Narratives About Women

Bonfield, Lynn A., and Mary C. Morrison. *Roxana's Children: The Biography of a Nineteenth-Century Vermont Family.* Amherst: University of Massachusetts Press, 1995.

Brumgardt, John R, ed. *Civil War Nurse: The Diary and Letters of Hannah Ropes.* Knoxville: University of Tennessee Press, 1980.

Buel, Joy Day, and Richard Buel Jr. *The Way of Duty: A Woman and Her Family in Revolutionary America.* New York: W.W. Norton, 1984.

deButts, Mary Custis Lee, ed. *Growing Up in the 1850s: The Journal of Agnes Lee.* Chapel Hill: University of North Carolina Press, 1984.

Eckhardt, Celia Morris. *Fanny Wright: Rebel in America.* Cambridge: Harvard University Press, 1984.

Hamburger, Lotte, and Joseph Hamburger. *Contemplating Adultery: The Secret Life of a Victorian Woman.* New York: Fawcett Columbine, 1991.

Lerner, Gerda. *The Grimke Sisters From South Carolina: Pioneers for Woman's Rights and Abolition.* New York: Schocken Books, 1971.

Logue, Mary. *Halfway Home: A Granddaughter's Biography.* St. Paul: Minnesota Historical Society Press, 1996.

Martinello, Marian L., with Ophelia Nielsen Weinheimer. *The Search for Emma's Story: A Model for Humanities Detective Work.* Fort Worth: Texas Christian University Press, 1987.

Moore, John Hammond, ed. *A Plantation Mistress on the Eve of the Civil War: The Diary of Keziah Goodwyn Hopkins Brevard, 1860–1861.* Columbia: University of South Carolina Press, 1993.

Nagel, Paul C. *The Adams Women: Abigail and Louisa Adams, Their Sisters and Daughters.* New York: Oxford University Press, 1987.

Schwartz, Gerald, ed. *A Woman Doctor's Civil War: Esther Hill Hawks' Diary.*

Columbia: University of South Carolina Press, 1984.

Sklar, Kathryn Kish. *Catharine Beecher: A Study in American Domesticity*. New Haven: Yale University Press, 1973.

Taves, Ann, ed. *Religion and Domestic Violence in Early New England: The Memoirs of Abigail Abbot Bailey*. Bloomington: Indiana University Press, 1989.

Ulrich, Laurel Thatcher. *A Midwife's Tale: The Life of Martha Ballard, Based on Her Diary, 1785–1812*. New York: Vintage Books, 1991.

Woodward, C. Vann, ed. *Mary Chesnut's Civil War*. New Haven: Yale University Press, 1981.

Works Cited in Case Studies

Cemetries of Harrison Township, Gallia County, Ohio. Gallipolis, Ohio: Gallia County Historical Society, 1980.

Chapin, Gilbert Warren. *The Chapin Book of Genealogical Data*. Hartford, Conn.: Chapin Family Association, 1924.

Chapin, Henry Millar. "The English Ancestry of Dea. Samuel Chapin of Springfield, Mass." *New England Historical and Genealogical Register* 83 (July 1929): 352–54.

———. *Life of Deacon Samuel Chapin, of Springfield*. Providence: Snow and Farnham Co., 1908.

Davis, Richard Beale, ed. *William Fitzhugh and His Chesapeake World, 1676–1701: The Fitzhugh Letters and Other Documents*. Chapel Hill: University of North Carolina Press, 1963.

Easton, William Starr. *Descendants of Joseph Easton, Hartford, Connecticut, 1636–1899*. St. Paul, Minn.: n.p., 1899.

Evans, Henrietta C., and Mary P. Wood. *Abstracts of Gallia County Chancery Records, 1835–52*. Privately pubilshed, 1984.

Fitzhugh, Marie. *Three Centuries Passed: The Fitzhugh Family*. San Antonio, Tex.: The Naylor Co., 1975.

French, Emily. *Emily: The Diary of a Hard-Worked Woman*. Ed. Janet Lecompte. Lincoln: University of Nebraska Press, 1987.

Gambino, Richard. *Blood of My Blood: The Dilemma of the Italian-Americans*. Garden City, N.Y.: Anchor Press, 1974.

Genealogies of Virginia Families From the Virginia Magazine of History and Biography. Vol. 2. Baltimore: Genealogical Publishing Co., 1981.

Hardy, Stella Pickett. *Colonial Families of the Southern States of America*. Baltimore: Genealogical Publishing Co., 1968.

Hart, Lyndon H. *A Guide to Bible Records in the Archives Branch, Virginia State Library*. Richmond: Virginia State Library, 1985.

Hosmer, James Kendall. *Winthop's Journal: "History of New England" 1630–1649*. New York: Charles Schribner's Sons, 1908.

Klein, Margaret C. *Tombstone Inscriptions of King George County, Virginia*. Baltimore: Genealogical Publishing Co., 1979.

Kukla, Jon. *Speakers and Clerks of the Virginia House of Burgesses, 1643–1776*. Richmond: Virginia State Library, 1981.

Perkins, Ruth, and Judy Froggett, comps. *Minister's Certificates of Marriages Commencing the Sixth Day of Sept. Anno 1836*. Greensburg, Ky.: Green County Library, 1984.

Records and Files of the Quarterly Courts of Essex County, Massachusetts, 1680–1683. Salem, Mass.: Essex Institute, 1921.

Schlegel, Donald M. *Franklin County, Ohio, Divorces Before 1870*. Columbus, Ohio: Columbus History Service, 1983.

Williams, Phyllis H. *South Italian Folkways in Europe and America: A Handbook for Social Workers, Visiting Nurses, School Teachers, and Physicians*. New Haven: Yale University Press, 1938.

Wright, Barbara. *Green County, Kentucky, Will Records, Book III, 1840–1875*. Privately published.

Writing and Publishing Guides

Crane, Madilyn Coen. "Numbering Your Genealogy—Special Cases: Surname Changes, Step Relationships, and Adoptions." *National Genealogical Society Quarterly* 83, no. 2 (June 1995): 84–95.

Curran, Joan Ferris. "Numbering Your Genealogy: Sound and Simple Systems." *National Genealogical Society Quarterly* 79, no. 3 (September 1991): 183–93.

Franklin, Jon. *Writing for Story: Craft Secrets of Dramatic Nonfiction*. New York: Atheneum, 1986.

Gerard, Philip. *Creative Nonfiction: Researching and Crafting Stories of Real Life*. Cincinnati: Story Press, 1996.

Gouldrup, Lawrence P. *Writing the Family Narrative*. Salt Lake City: Ancestry Publishing, 1987.

———. *Writing the Family Narrative Workbook*. Salt Lake City: Ancestry Publishing, 1993.

Hatcher, Patricia Law. *Producing a Quality Family History*. Salt Lake City: Ancestry Publishing, 1996.

Heilbrun, Carolyn G. *Writing a Woman's Life*. New York: W.W. Norton, 1988.

Hughes, Ann Hege. "Preparing Manuscripts for Offset Printing." *Association of Professional Genealogists Quarterly* 8 (June 1993): 31–33.

———. "Publishing Genealogical Research: Commercially and Privately." *Association of Professional Genealogists Quarterly* 5 (fall 1990): 60–62.

McCutcheon, Marc. *The Writer's Guide to Everyday Life From Prohibition Through World War II*. Cincinnati: Writer's Digest Books, 1995.

———. *The Writer's Guide to Everyday Life in the 1800s.* Cincinnati: Writer's Digest Books, 1993.

Polking, Kirk. *Writing Family Histories and Memoirs.* Cincinnati: Betterway Books, 1995.

Poynter, Dan. *The Self-Publishing Manual: How to Write, Print, and Sell Your Own Book.* 8th ed. Santa Barbara: Para Publishing, 1995.

Sturdevant, Katherine Scott. "Documentary Editing for Family Historians." *Association of Professional Genealogists Quarterly* 5 (fall 1990): 51–57.

Taylor, Dale. *The Writer's Guide to Everyday Life in Colonial America, From 1607–1783.* Cincinnati: Writer's Digest Books, 1997.

Wray, John H. "Numbering Your Genealogy: Multiple Immigrants and Non-Emigrating Collaterals." *National Genealogical Society Quarterly* 85 (March 1997): 39–47.

INDEX